T0310540

Valuing Businesses Using Regression Analysis

A Quantitative Approach to the Guideline Company Transaction Method

C. FRED HALL, III

WILEY

Library of Congress Cataloging-in-Publication Data is avaiable:

ISBN 9781119793427 (hardback)
ISBN 9781119793441 (epdf)
ISBN 9781119793434 (epub)

Cover Design: Wiley
Cover Image: © C. Fred Hall, III

SKY10026028_040621

To the two great ladies in my life; my bride of nearly 50 years, Joanie, who has proofread every one of my 800 valuations and is still talking to me. She probably knows more about valuations than most of the professionals in the industry. Due to her great life experiences of having worked with many CPAs and attorneys, she has a gift of being able to read complicated text and then help me to rewrite it in plain English. She has made me look a whole lot better than I am.

To my mother, Connie, who for the last five years has constantly given me encouragement to write this book. She was so happy to hear that the dream was going to become a reality. Unfortunately, she passed away at 99 years just before it was published.

Contents

Foreword

As an executive and entrepreneur for the last 30 years, I have been regularly involved in business development, marketing, business brokerage, and business valuations. Every new project, it seemed, started with a valuation of the business. For years I did my own valuations. However, I was continually frustrated with how the different multiplier methodologies produced widely divergent values. Convention had us average the different values, but I never had confidence in the resulting value. Needless to say, when presenting my findings to the owner of the business, he or she would notice that one or two of the methodologies produced a very high value compared to the other values. The question always arose as to why I was not using the higher value.

I also worked with many potential buyers of businesses. When I would show them my research on the estimate of value, they would, of course, focus on the lower values. Suffice to say, conventional methodologies often brought up more questions than answers and, as such, never satisfied anyone. Five years ago I was introduced to C. Fred Hall, III. He explained to me why the different methodologies produced such different values. It made sense. I decided to use him to value my clients' businesses rather than doing so myself. In the last five years we have collaborated on over 100 deals; more than 80 of them required valuations.

When taking a business to market, the asking price must be reasonable or potential buyers will never respond. The values produced by Fred's methodology were spot on. We had very few credible challenges on the asking prices by either buyers or sellers. Another aspect to Fred's approach is to ensure we are comparing like-kind businesses that are "performing at the same level as the sellers." Sellers appreciate this type of comparison vs. using a typical average multiple for an industry. Fred's method can appear complicated, but the charts produced by the regressions to determine the appropriate multipliers for the company are so compelling that there is little one can argue about. Anyone involved in business valuations needs to adopt Fred's methodology. It works!

I should mention that as a result of the businesses being properly valued, I was able to close far more deals. In 2017 the International Business Brokers Association honored me with the Chairman's Circle Award as one of the top producing brokers in the United States. In 2018 and 2019 I was awarded "Outstanding Producer" honors as well. Fred's valuation methodology has been a big part of our success!

Randy Hendershot,
CEO of Evolution Advisors,
CBB

After finishing my MBA, I went to work for a major west coast bank. I chose the bank because it had one of the top management training programs in the industry. This was important to me because I felt that my MBA training left me clueless about businesses. I was right. The bank's management training program was an intense nine-month, 40-hours-a-week class, on analyzing businesses. It was equivalent to a second MBA degree. Upon completion of the training I was confident that I now understood businesses. I was wrong. It wasn't until I owned my own business (I must clarify that my wife and I owned it) that some of the lights went on. However, it wasn't until we sold that business after 27 years and I then went to work as a business broker for a major brokerage firm in northern California that I began to really understand businesses.

MBA education was largely theoretical in those days, and banking was the technical application of that theory. However, owning your own business teaches you many things you would never learn in school: that education is largely on the fly. As a sole proprietor, your skillset, for the most part, is self-taught, and class is in session 60 hours a week for the entire period of ownership. I thought all that knowledge was unique and original. However, after 18 years of being a business broker and business appraiser and having worked with over 800 business owners, I find that we all seemed to think alike. We made similar choices and similar mistakes.

When I was considering selling my business, my first choice of potential buyers was my general manager. He worked for me for over 20 years. He was very loyal and made me a lot of money. I thought I owed him the opportunity to buy my business. This was me being an incredibly generous person. Come to find out, every owner thinks like this. In actuality it was not an act of generosity or loyalty on my part. It was my desire to create the simplest exit strategy whereby I could get the price I wanted for the business without any negotiations.

Sadly, once the excitement of buying my company wore off, my manager realized he didn't have the money or the intestinal fortitude to run an $8 million business with 30 employees. He subsequently declined my offer, and a few months later he quit because he felt that he had failed in my eyes. I was more disappointed in this decision than he was; I lost the best employee I ever had.

Over the last 18 years I have worked with hundreds of business owners wanting to sell their businesses. I found that the majority of them approached their managers first. Not only were few owners successful, but amazingly, most reported that their manager subsequently quit as well. In many of those cases where the owner and manager actually reached an agreement, the bank appraisal for the acquisition loan came in significantly lower than the seller wanted, thus killing the deal. The owner never considered getting an appraisal for the business. The asking price was based on the amount needed for retirement, not what the business was worth.

The second mistake sellers frequently make when selling their businesses may appear to have little to do with the value of the businesses. However, I mention it because owners should approach this choice with extreme caution. After I was unsuccessful selling my business to my manager, I felt that one of my competitors was the next most logical suitor. In retrospect, it was my desire to create the easiest exit strategy and maximize my selling price. The competitor would certainly be aware of the many strengths of my business. In addition, there would not be a need for training, thus, providing me with a quick exit. The owner would also want my business so badly, he or she would pay any amount that I asked, and, of course, the owner had the deep pockets to pay that price. Again, the actual value of the business did not enter into my decision.

The result of my decision to approach my competitor turned out to be textbook—I've seen it happen many times over the last 18 years. It never occurred to me that there are unscrupulous business owners out there. The manager of my competitor knew I took Mondays off. He came into the store on my day off and passed out business cards to all my employees. He told them that when I sold the store, the buyer would be so strapped with debt payments they would not get pay raises for years. Their best choice was to come work for him. The manager then sent his sales force out to all my customers and told them that I was leaving and he was now the best choice of suppliers. I lost employees and customers, which impacted the value of my business.

Just make sure that when you approach a competitor, have him or her sign a non-disclosure agreement that has significant penalties for talking to your employees, customers, suppliers, or other competitors.

In addition, no matter who the potential buyer may be, ask a price that is fair and reasonable. Buyers are not dumb. If they feel that the asking price is not reasonable, they will not try to negotiate. They will simply walk away. You will call, text, and email, but believe me, they will not respond. You will have no idea that the reason they stopped communicating was that your price was too high. As a business broker, I have seen this happen hundreds of times.

Hence, one of the main concerns of all business owners should be, "What is my business worth?" As a business owner, I relied on business brokers and CPAs for information on the value of my business. As a business broker, the most common question I was asked was, "What is the multiplier for my business?" The assumption of most business owners is that a single multiplier exists for his or her type of business that can be applied to its level of profits in order to determine the value of the business. The assumption follows that as an appraiser, I can merely open a textbook on business multipliers and give the owner an answer in a few seconds. If business appraisals were that simple, we would all be out of work and Wall Street would be nonexistent.

After many years of research on the subject, I find that every business is unique and will have its own set of multipliers. Those multipliers are derived from the company's level of profitability and revenue. Hence, I am incredulous to find business brokers and business consultants who offer up multipliers to their clients without even knowing what the company's level of revenue and profits are and how they compare to the competition.

Unfortunately, there are a few industry textbooks on rules of thumb, which are collections of thousands of brokers' opinions of the multipliers for hundreds of business classifications. These "rules of thumb" books are used extensively by brokers to estimate the value of their client's business. The textbooks, however, should not be used as a substitute for a quantitative business analysis and valuation. To do so would quite possibly over- or undervalue a business 10 to 20%. For a million-dollar business, 20% is a significant sum of money. If the business is overvalued, it may result in an unsuccessful attempt to sell the business.

The saddest case in which I was involved was a business where an unseasoned business broker had recommended a $1 million listing price based on some rule of thumb. The owners were a couple in their 70s who wanted to retire. After wasting a year and a half waiting for an offer that never materialized, they called on me to value the business. I determined that their business was worth only $500,000. The couple was convinced (or should I say, hoped) the broker was right and refused to accept my opinion. They spent another year and a half trying to sell the business. During that time, the husband passed away and the wife ultimately sold the business for roughly what I had appraised it. The couple wasted over three years and never got to enjoy retirement together.

PEER REVIEWING THE REGRESSION METHODOLOGY

A question I frequently am asked when presenting my regression methodology is, "Will this procedure pass a Daubert challenge?" A Daubert challenge is a hearing in a court of law in which the validity and admissibility of expert testimony is challenged by opposing counsel. Even if the method used by the expert appears to be scientifically sound and reasonable, the fact that it has not been vetted by the industry peers may lead to it being thrown out of court.

I am not an attorney or a judge, but my response would be, "Yes, my methodology would survive a Daubert challenge." During the last eight years, I have written over 400 appraisals using the regression methodology. Half those valuations were for partnership splits or divorces, many of which involved contentious partners and their attorneys. I have submitted over 100 appraisals to eight different banks in northern California for their SBA loans. I have also submitted a dozen valuations to the IRS for estate valuations or gifting purposes. Out of all those valuations, I have not received a single credible challenge. As you will see later in this book, the methodology is so compelling that it is difficult to find an issue to challenge.

More importantly, my regression methodology has been published in most of the industry's leading trade journals including:

IBA's (Institute of Business Appraisers) "Business Appraisal Practice," second quarter 2012

Business Valuation Resources – "Best of 2012—What's It Worth?"

NACVA's (National Association of Certified Valuators and Analysts) "Value Examiner," July 2016

Thomson-Reuter's "Valuation Strategies," July 2016

NACVA's "Quick Read," January 2018

I have also presented the methodology at five NACVA national conferences: June 2016, December 2017, June 2018, June 2020, and August 2020.

Lastly, in January 2017 Jim Hitchner reviewed my methodology in his annual "Current Updates in Valuations" and gave it "two thumbs up." Mr. Hitchner is one of the industry's leading educators.

WHY ISN'T EVERYONE USING THIS METHODOLOGY?

A very good question! Appraisers are slow to change their methodologies especially when the new ones are not an "easy sell." For example, an expert can stand in front of a jury and state that he or she used the median revenue and cash flow multipliers to determine the value of the subject business. He or she would go on to say, "Median is the measure of central tendency that shows us where the market is." Everyone has been exposed to the term "median" as it is used extensively in the real estate industry. Hence, the entire jury panel would be nodding their heads up and down in approval. However, if the expert were to stand in front of the jury and state that "Regression is the root-mean-square measure of dispersion about the...," everyone would immediately fall asleep. Unfortunately, there are a few judges out there who consider regression as "voodoo statistics."

Regression on the surface is a very complex statistical tool. When I was in my MBA program, I enrolled in an advanced forecasting economics class. (This was before personal computers and copy machines when dinosaurs roamed the earth.) On the first day of class the teacher walked in with a large binder under his arm and announced that we were all going to learn regression in his class. The chalkboard at the front of the classroom was 20 feet wide and the chalkboard on the side wall was also 20 feet wide. He proceeded to write the formula for linear regression on the chalkboard. It completely covered both chalkboards. I spent the next three months in the university's computer lab typing the formula on punched paper IBM cards.

Luckily, today we can accomplish the same task with a click of a button with Microsoft Excel's regression utility. In several chapters we will go through all the steps one must take to use Excel's regression in my methodology. More importantly, I will break down regression into its very simple components. I will produce charts that are so compelling that anyone looking at the chart will realize that medians are *not* the measure of central tendency of where the market is—regression is. Hence, if you are facing an opposing expert in court, you can easily discredit his or her methodology by showing these charts.

I will be spending a significant portion of this book demonstrating Excel's regression in order for the reader to obtain a better understanding of how it works and to be able to replicate the methodology. However, at the conclusion of the book I will introduce a template that will accomplish the entire methodology in seconds with the click of a button.

Acknowledgments

NATIONAL ASSOCIATION OF CERTIFIED VALUATORS AND ANALYSTS (NACVA)

Portions of Chapter 1 and Chapter 2 have been published in NACVA's "The Value Examiner" in the July/August 2016 issue, p. 16. Portions of Chapter 8 have been published in NACVA's "Quick Read," in the January 2018 issue, p. 5.

Portions of Chapter 1 and Chapter 2 have been recorded in nationally televised live presentations at five different NACVA conferences: June 2016, December 2017, June 2018, June 2020, and August 2020.

NACVA has granted the author and John Wiley and Sons, Inc. permission to publish the above-mentioned material in this book.

INSTITUTE OF BUSINESS APPRAISERS (IBA, A SUBSIDIARY OF NACVA)

Portions of Chapter 1 and Chapter 2 have been published in IBA's "Business Appraisal Practice" in the Second Quarter 2012 issue, p. 18.

Portions of Chapter 8 have been published in IBA's "Business Appraisal Practice" in the First Quarter 2014 issue, p. 15.

NACVA has granted the author and John Wiley and Sons, Inc. permission to publish the above-mentioned material in this book.

THOMSON-REUTERS CORPORATION

Portions of Chapter 1 and Chapter 2 have been published in Thomson-Reuters' "Valuation Strategies" in the July 2016 issue, p. 30.

Thomson-Reuters has granted the author and John Wiley and Sons, Inc. permission to publish the above-mentioned material in this book.

BUSINESS VALUATION RESOURCES, LLC (BVR)

Portions of Chapter 1 and Chapter 2 have been published in BVR's "What It's Worth" in the April 2012 issue, p. 1 and reprinted in the July 2012 issue, p. 30.

Business Valuation Resources has granted the author and John Wiley and Sons, Inc. permission to publish the above-mentioned material in this book.

Current Methodologies

The Guideline Company Transaction Method is a subset of the Market Approach and is a sister to the Guideline Public Company Method. The two methods are characterized by the transactional databases used in the calculation of value. The Guideline Public Company Method uses various SEC (Securities and Exchange Commission) data of publicly traded companies that have been acquired by other publicly traded companies. This method is obviously used to value large-sized publicly traded corporations. The Guideline Company Transaction Method, which will be used in this book, references a number of subscription-based databases that have recorded the sales of small privately owned companies. The data from those transactions is compared to the subject company in order to draw a conclusion of its value.

The focus of the regression methodology being presented is primarily on companies with revenue less than $5 million. Most of those transactions have been handled by main street business brokers. Most of these business brokers have been schooled by the IBBA (International Business Brokers Association) and therefore, present the transactional data using the same format. As companies increase in size, especially those with revenues greater than $10 million, M&A specialists (mergers and acquisitions) are the more common sales agents. These larger companies are referred to as middle-market businesses—bigger than main street but smaller than Wall Street. The M&A professionals analyze financial statements differently than main street brokers. For the most part they use EBITDA (Earnings Before Interest, Taxes, Depreciation, and Amortization) as a measure of earnings rather than SDE (Seller's Discretionary Earnings). The two values are significantly different as are the rules to calculate them.

The terms Seller's Discretionary Earnings (SDE) and cash flow will be used interchangeably throughout this book.

There are several transactional databases available that concentrate on the smaller main street businesses. The four databases referenced in this book are:

1. DealStats (formerly Pratt's Stats) has over 30,000 transactions. The median revenue of all the transactions is $750,000. 75% generated less than $3,500,000 in revenue. Most of the data is obtained from business broker submissions. However, for many of the larger transactions the data was harvested from SEC filings of 8-K quarterly financial reports. The database is owned and managed by Business Valuation Resources, LLC, Portland, Oregon.

2. Bizcomps® has over 14,000 transactions with a median revenue of $455,000. 75% generated less than $915,000 in revenue. All the transactional data is obtained from broker submissions. The database was created by Jack Sanders and is owned by Bizcomps Services, Las Vegas, Nevada.

3. ValuSource (formerly IBA) has over 42,000 transactions with a median revenue of $341,000. 75% generated less than $766,000 in revenue. All transactional data is obtained from broker submissions. The database is owned by ValuSource, Colorado Springs, Colorado.

4. Peercomps has over 10,000 transactions with a median revenue of $1,034,000. 75% generated less than $1,890,000 in revenue. Data is obtained from SBA lending banks. The database is owned by Peercomps, Inc., Lutz, Florida.

A notable fifth database is ValuSource M&A Comps (formerly DoneDeals), which provides transactions in the private-sector middle-market (companies with revenues from $10 million to $300 million or more). Most of its transactions are much larger than the $3 to $5 million range of the other four databases. The regression methodology advanced in this book has not been tested on this larger population of privately held businesses.

Each of the four main databases report transactional data in slightly different formats. However, there typically is enough data to reconcile each transaction to yield a selling price in an asset sale value format. An asset sale is the most common structure in which small businesses are sold. The owner only sells the company's inventory, fixtures and equipment, and its intangibles (goodwill, covenant-not-to-compete, etc.) and retains the business entity, cash, and accounts receivable and pays off all the liabilities.

Each transaction used in the regression methodology must be reconciled to an Asset Sale Value so that they will be directly comparable.

The procedural manuals of the four databases also indicate minor differences in the way revenue and discretionary earnings are reported. DealStats collects 165 data points for each transaction including a summary of the P&L and balance sheet, a description of the terms of the deal, the type of consideration tendered, and whether it is a stock sale or an asset sale. Because of the extensive information available, reconciling Seller's Discretionary Cash Flow or reconciling the actual selling price of the transaction is often more reliable. DealStats calculates SDE similarly to Bizcomps and ValuSource; however, it is not uncommon to find discrepancies among all three. Careful analysis of all the databases will help avoid selecting incorrect transactional data. The greater detail offered by the DealStats database can help reduce errors in selecting the transactional data. Therefore, if there are any discrepancies arising among duplicate transactions reported by the databases, the DealStats data will generally be used in the analysis.

Nevertheless, in instances where the databases reported the same transaction, I have found that in a high percentage of the cases the selling price, gross revenues, and discretionary earnings were similar. In instances where there were differences, the available data often enabled one to reconcile the values to be comparable. One can attribute this similarity to the fact that the same brokers will report a transaction to all three databases (Peercomps only uses bank data) and will offer only one calculation for selling price and Seller's Discretionary Earnings (SDE). Brokers will typically follow the convention recommended by the IBBA (International Business Brokers Association) for calculating SDE. Therefore, all of the databases will be considered similar enough in their respective construction to be grouped together. Shannon Pratt draws the same conclusion in *The Market Approach to Valuing Businesses*.[1]

> *"One may combine the data from the three databases into a single table. [However,] the analyst must be aware of and make certain adjustments to reflect that the three databases do not define the underlying financial variables in exactly the same way."*

PROCEDURES USED IN THE GUIDELINE COMPANY TRANSACTION METHOD

Gross Revenue Multiplier

This method is a simple ratio of a company's selling price divided by its gross revenues. Companies within a specific industry classification have a tendency to exhibit similar relationships between their revenues and selling price. Selling

---

[1]Shannon Pratt, *The Market Approach to Valuing Businesses*, Hoboken, NJ: John Wiley and Sons, 2001, p. 68.

price and gross revenues of a company are readily obtainable, making this method easy to apply. However, it does not consider the company's profitability or asset valuation in the equation. Therefore, this method, if used by itself, may produce a misread of a company's potential value. The method also does not conform to IRS ruling 59-60 that states one's methodologies must be based on cash flow.

Cash Flow Multiplier

This method is the ratio of a company's selling price divided by its Seller's Discretionary Earnings (SDE). It should be noted that the database sources used in the Guideline Company Transaction Method calculate earnings differently than the way we calculated net cash flow in the Income Approach. SDE is calculated by removing one owner's salary and perquisites (such as health and pension benefits or personal autos) from expenses. Interest, depreciation, income taxes, any one-time expense or income, and any non-operating expense or income are also removed from the income statement. The process of calculating SDE from a company's financial statements is referred to as "recasting." Recasting will be discussed in depth in the following pages.

However, one of the same problems with the gross revenue multiplier exists with the cash flow multiplier. That is, the ratio only focuses on one aspect of the company's operations—its discretionary earnings. Therefore, if used by itself, this ratio may produce a misread of the company's value. For that reason, the Market Approach typically includes both the cash flow and gross revenue multipliers to estimate the value of a business.

Enterprise Value + Inventory

Under certain circumstances, however, using the earlier two methodologies can still produce inaccurate results when valuing businesses that derive the bulk of their revenues from the sale of inventory. For example, it was determined that the average hardware store sells for 0.45 times its gross revenue and 3.30 times its SDE. In our search, we find two guideline companies, each generating $900,000 in gross revenues and $125,000 in SDE; yet one sold for $400,000 and the second for $600,000. The anomaly can probably be explained by the fact that the first store had $200,000 in inventory while the second had $400,000.

The enterprise value + inventory methodology deducts the volatile inventory component from the selling price of the business. The difference is then divided by the company's SDE. The resulting ratio can be used to determine what is referred to as the enterprise value of the business; that is, the value of a business excluding its inventory. By using this methodology on the two transactions above, we find that enterprise value for both businesses was 1.60 [Store #1 = ($400,000 – $200,000) ÷ $125,000; Store #2 = ($600,000 – $400,000) ÷ $125,000]. We can then use this ratio to estimate the value of a third hardware store that generated, say, $1,450,000 in gross revenues, $200,000 in SDE, and had $375,000 in inventory. Store #3's enterprise value is $320,000 ($200,000 × 1.60); its total value including inventory is, therefore, $320,000 + $375,000, or $695,000. The cash flow multiplier by itself would have predicted only $660,000 (3.30 × $200,000) and the gross revenue multiplier would have predicted $652,500 (0.45 × $1,450,000).

When reconciling the above three market value multipliers to estimate the value of this third hardware store, we might consider giving additional weighting to the enterprise value because this store primarily generates its revenue from the sale of inventory.

Recasting

The "recasting" of a company's earnings serves two purposes. First, the databases we use for comparables are a collection of all forms of business entities: S corporations, C corporations, LLCs, partnerships, and proprietorships. Hence, we need to strip away the differences in accounting methods used by each of those different entity types in order to make them directly comparable. For example, sole proprietorships (SP) report earnings on the Schedule C of the owner's personal tax return. There is no owner's salary expense in an SP; the "bottom line" represents the owner's total income, and payroll taxes for that income appears on the owner's 1040. However, corporations and partnerships generally include a deduction for an owner's salary expense including payroll taxes on that salary. Thus, the bottom line for these entities is net of the owner's salary and payroll taxes. To make the corporate tax return earnings line up with the SP, we would have to add back the owner's salary and payroll tax.

Health benefits are a deduction in C corporations but not in SPs (benefits appear on the owner's 1040). Many accountants also do not include owner's health benefits in S corporations, opting to deduct them on the owner's 1040 tax return. Donations are usually a deduction in C corporations but often not in S corporations (donations frequently appear on the owner's K-1). Accelerated depreciation (IRC Section 179) and gains or losses from the sale of assets often do not appear on an S corporation tax return (they often appear on the owner's K-1) but do on a C corporation or on an SP. State income taxes do not appear on an SP but do on a corporation. SPs by definition have one owner, whereas corporations and partnerships may have multiple owners, all with salaries that are expensed, thereby reducing the bottom line. Finally, since interest expense can vary greatly between similar companies, making direct comparisons of earnings is difficult. Thus, it is also common practice to remove interest expense from the recast financials.

In order to develop some measure of earnings for all these different entities that are directly comparable to each other, the databases have removed all those accounting differences from their income statements. Accordingly, each entity's reported "earnings" is net of taxes, depreciation, health benefits, donations, capital gains, interest expense, and most importantly, net of just one owner's salary and payroll tax. The resulting measure of earnings is referred to as "Seller's Discretionary Earnings" (SDE).

If a company has multiple owners (including working spouses of owners), the salary of the principal owner who would most likely be replaced by a hypothetical buyer is added back to discretionary earnings (SDE). It is also assumed that the hypothetical buyer would have to replace all the secondary owners or family members with hired employees. Consequently, all owners' and family members' salaries are added back to SDE, but the replacement costs of the secondary owners and family members are *deducted* from SDE.

If the present owner is an absentee owner, the salary of the general manager is added back to SDE along with the owner's salary. The assumption here is that a hypothetical buyer will be a full-time operating owner/manager, thereby replacing both the manager and the owner. In doing so he will earn the manager's salary and the owner's salary.

After applying all the above appropriate adjustments, we can then directly compare the recast Sellers Discretionary Earnings of corporations to sole proprietorships, partnerships, and so on. (The terms "Seller's Discretionary Earnings" and "cash flow" are used interchangeably in the following Market Approach discussion.)

The second purpose for recasting a company's earnings is to attempt to present a normalized view of the subject company's operations. The recast financials should serve as a proxy for the level of operations from which we may reasonably expect future revenues to evolve. Thus, we select an earnings period that best represents the current level of operations (which may not be the current year's P&Ls), and then we remove any non-operating income or expenses and any non-recurring income or expenses. The result should be an income stream for the subject company that we can reasonably expect under normal circumstances. The normalized P&L of the subject has now been properly recast and can be compared to the database guideline companies.

Conventional Analysis of a Sample of Comparables

After a sample of transactions has been selected, the typical approach is to use various statistical measures to calculate the appropriate multipliers that we discussed previously. Exhibit 1.1 shows a sample of transactions with the revenue and cash flow multipliers calculated for each. At the bottom of the table, three different metrics were used to calculate appropriate multipliers to be applied to the subject's revenue and cash flow to determine the estimated value of the business—lower quartile, median, and upper quartile.[2]

One of the current popular topics regarding Market Approach methodologies is whether the median or the harmonic mean is the better statistical measure to calculate the revenue and cash flow multipliers of a sample of comparables. Both metrics have their strong points. However, the multipliers they generate occasionally produce values for an appraisal subject that do not appear reasonable. It is fairly common that the value calculated using the median revenue multiplier of a sample of comparables is considerably higher than the value calculated using the median cash flow multiplier. And, at other times, we find that the value calculated using the median cash flow multiplier is considerably higher than the value using the median revenue multiplier.

The Problem

We will start with a typical sample of comparables that an appraiser might collect. Exhibit 1.1 shows 24 companies that were similar to our subject company.

Each transaction shows the selling price, gross revenue, cash flow, and its calculated revenue and cash flow multipliers. From the data we can calculate the median revenue multiplier

---

[2]Many appraisers also use a wider range of revenue and cash flow by calculating the standard deviation or tenth percentile of earnings and revenue.

EXHIBIT 1.1 Sample of Transactional Data

	Selling Price (b)	Gross Revenue (c)	Cash Flow (SDE) (d)	Rev. Mult. (b) ÷ (c)	CF Mult. (b) ÷ (d)
1	170,000	1,250,000	37,000	0.14	4.66
2	252,000	1,405,000	49,000	0.18	5.14
3	315,000	1,193,000	83,000	0.26	3.81
4	300,000	1,291,000	90,000	0.23	3.33
5	312,000	1,278,000	94,000	0.24	3.32
6	509,000	1,175,000	97,000	0.43	5.25
7	575,000	1,225,000	115,000	0.47	5.00
8	575,000	1,200,000	103,000	0.48	5.58
9	347,000	1,120,000	105,000	0.31	3.30
10	430,000	1,345,000	142,000	0.32	3.03
11	575,000	1,386,000	151,000	0.41	3.81
12	550,000	1,376,000	168,000	0.40	3.27
13	690,000	1,017,000	126,000	0.68	5.46
14	568,000	1,183,000	157,000	0.48	3.63
15	391,000	1,255,000	178,000	0.31	2.20
16	520,000	1,282,000	186,000	0.41	2.80
17	275,000	1,172,000	171,000	0.23	1.61
18	594,000	1,315,000	203,000	0.45	2.93
19	700,000	1,176,000	215,000	0.59	3.26
20	565,000	1,049,000	172,000	0.54	3.29
21	577,000	1,280,000	213,000	0.45	2.71
22	650,000	1,050,000	210,000	0.62	3.10
23	545,000	1,017,000	204,000	0.54	2.67
24	700,000	1,250,000	275,000	0.56	2.55
	Price	Revenue	Cash Flow	Rev. Mult. Range	CF Mult. Range
Avg	$487,000	$1,220,000	$148,000	0.41	3.57
		Lower Quartile =		0.30	2.89
		Median =		0.42	3.30
		Upper Quartile =		0.49	4.02

for the whole sample (0.42) and the median cash flow multiplier (3.30). We also note that the average company sold for $487,000 and had an average revenue of $1,220,000 and cash flow of $148,000.

Our first example valuation using the data from Exhibit 1.1 will be for a company that is fairly similar to the average-sized comparable in our sample. The subject's revenue was $1,200,000, and its cash flow was $150,000.

By using the median revenue multiplier of 0.42 from Exhibit 1.1 we obtain an estimated value for our subject of $504,000. The median cash flow multiplier produces a value of $495,000. The values from both metrics are reasonably similar and no one would challenge the appraiser for opining a value of $500,000.

EXHIBIT 1.1

	Price	Revenue	Cash Flow	Rev. Mult. Range	CF Mult. Range
Avg	$487,000	$1,220,000	$148,000	0.41	3.57
		Lower Quartile =		0.30	2.89
		Median =		0.42	3.30
		Upper Quartile =		0.49	4.02

EXHIBIT 1.2　Average-Performing Subject Company

Example #1
Average-Performing Subject Company:
Revenue　　　　　　$1,200,000
Cash Flow　　　　　$150,000
Median Revenue Multiplier Value
$1,200,000 × 0.42 = $504,000
Median Cash Flow Multiplier Value
$150,000 × 3.30 = $495,000
Opinion of Value is: $500.000

The use of medians begins to have problems when we appraise a company that is an underperformer. Example #2 below is one such company where revenues are the same as example #1, but its cash flow is only $85,000, far less than the $148,000 average of our sample. The median revenue multiplier of 0.42 from Exhibit 1.1a produces the same value for this unprofitable company as the more profitable company in example #1. As such, we know that isn't a reasonable value.

The cash flow multiplier of 3.30 produces a value of $280,500, which appears to be too low.

EXHIBIT 1.1a

	Price	Revenue	Cash Flow	Rev. Mult. Range	CF Mult. Range
Avg	$487,000	$1,220,000	$148,000	0.41	3.57
Lower Quartile =				0.30	2.89
Median =				0.42	3.30
Upper Quartile =				0.49	4.02

EXHIBIT 1.3   Low-Profit Subject Company

Example #2

Low-Profit Subject Company:

    Revenue $1,200,000

    Cash Flow $ 85,000

Using Median Multiplier Values

    $1,200,000 × 0.42 = $504,000;

       $85,000 × 3.30 = $280,500;

OR: Which one is it?

Using Lower Quartile Values

    $1,200,000 × 0.30 = $360,000

       $85,000 × 2.89 = $245,650

Opinion of Value is: ?

If the appraiser decided to use the lower quartile of multipliers, using the justification that the subject is an underperformer, we find the revenue multiplier value was $360,000 ($1,200,000 × 0.30). Although that value would seem reasonable, given that the more profitable company in example #1 was worth $504,000, the lower-quartile cash flow multiplier produces a value of only $245,650 ($85,000 × 2.89). Since the appraiser ends up with four values that are so different, how does one know which one is reasonable or, for that matter, if even taking an average is appropriate?

EXHIBIT 1.1b Exhibit

	Price	Revenue	Cash Flow	Rev. Mult. Range	CF Mult. Range
Avg	$487,000	$1,220,000	$148,000	0.41	3.57
		Lower Quartile =		0.30	2.89
		Median =		0.42	3.30
		Upper Quartile =		0.49	4.02

EXHIBIT 1.4 High-Profit Subject Company

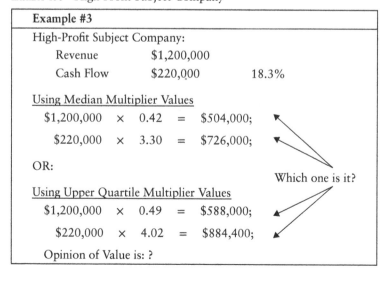

Example #3
High-Profit Subject Company:
Revenue $1,200,000
Cash Flow $220,000   18.3%
Using Median Multiplier Values
$1,200,000 × 0.42 = $504,000;
$220,000 × 3.30 = $726,000;
OR:
Which one is it?
Using Upper Quartile Multiplier Values
$1,200,000 × 0.49 = $588,000;
$220,000 × 4.02 = $884,400;
Opinion of Value is: ?

Example #3 shows a company that is far more profitable than the average company in our sample. The resulting cash flow multiplier values for this company are much higher than the revenue multiplier values, which is exactly the opposite situation that occurred with the unprofitable company in example #2.

Again, the median revenue multiplier of 0.42 produces the same value as the less profitable companies in examples #1 and #2, so we know that isn't a reasonable value. The cash flow multiplier of 3.30 produces a value of $726,000 ($220,000 × 3.3), which appears to be too high.

If the appraiser decided to use the upper quartile of multipliers, using the justification that the subject is an above-average performer, we find the revenue multiplier value was $588,000 ($1,200,000 × 0.49). Although that value would seem reasonable, the matching upper-quartile cash flow multiplier produces an unrealistically high value of $884,000 ($220,000 × 4.02). Once again, the appraiser ends up with four values that are so different, this scenario is wide open for challenge.

CHAPTER 2

The Solution

An appraiser or anyone reading an appraisal is only going to see a valuation for one company. Thus, one will not be aware that the values for an underperforming or over-performing subject are potentially way off the mark when using the median to calculate multipliers. Why are the values for companies that are at the opposite ends of the cash flow spectrum so divergent? Answer: Regardless of how profitable the subject company was, it was accorded the same median multipliers gleaned from the sample. In other words, median and quartiles are one-dimensional.

The solution is to add another dimension to the analysis.

IRS Revenue Ruling 59-60 instructs business appraisers to give considerable weighting to a company's profitability when determining its value.[1] As such we observe the subject's cash flow growth over the previous several years and identify all the drivers that created that growth. We also look at the subject's local market and how it will affect its operations and consider the prospects for its continued growth in the future. We then compared the subject's balance sheet and P&L ratios to a database of thousands of similar companies to determine

---

[1]Internal Revenue Service, Revenue Ruling 59-60, 1959, http://www.hantzmon wiebel.com/live_data/documents/ruling-59-60.pdf, section 5, p. 5.

the subject's relative strength compared to its peer group. The question is, then, once we have determined that our subject is better than its peer group, what is the market willing to pay for that distinction?

When trying to make a direct comparison of the subject to companies that have recently sold, the available databases of sold transactions do not provide us with much financial information. The only effective tool available is to compare each company's discretionary earnings profit margins (abbrev. SDE%). This simple ratio, Seller's Discretionary Earnings divided by gross revenues, gives us the means to directly compare the relative performance of companies in terms of their profitability and to observe how it affects the selling price of the business.

Generally speaking, when comparing companies of similar size and SIC code (Standard Industrial Classification), those that have higher SDE% tend to be the more dominant players within their markets. They can command higher prices for their products and services. They also control expenses more efficiently than their competition.

To determine the effect of a company's profitability on its selling price we begin by adding another column of data to our original sample in Exhibit 1.1. The column in Exhibit 2.1 contains the operating profit margins (SDE%) of each transaction. The formula for SDE% is: cash flow ÷ revenue.[2] Exhibit 2.1 has been sorted so that the least profitable companies, with the lowest SDE%, are at the top and the most profitable companies, with the highest SDE%, are at the bottom.

When we sort the data in this manner, we immediately notice that the companies with the lowest SDE% also tended to have the lowest revenue multipliers. For example, the five companies

---

[2]The measure of cash flow used in the examples is known as "Seller's Discretionary Earnings," or SDE. This is a measure most commonly used for valuations of smaller companies with revenues under $5 million. It is normalized EBITDA – one owner's total compensation. The operating profit margin using SDE is notated as SDE%.

Observ.	Selling Price (b)	Gross Revenue (c)	Cash Flow (SDE) (d)	SDE% (d) ÷ (c)	Rev. Mult. (b) ÷ (c)	CF Mult. (b) ÷ (d)
1	170,000	1,250,000	37,000	2.9%	0.14	4.66
2	252,000	1,405,000	49,000	3.5%	0.18	5.14
3	315,000	1,193,000	83,000	6.9%	0.26	3.81
4	300,000	1,291,000	90,000	7.0%	0.23	3.33
5	312,000	1,278,000	94,000	7.4%	0.24	3.32
6	509,000	1,175,000	97,000	8.3%	0.43	5.25
7	575,000	1,200,000	103,000	8.6%	0.48	5.58
8	347,000	1,120,000	105,000	9.4%	0.31	3.30
9	575,000	1,225,000	115,000	9.4%	0.47	5.00
10	430,000	1,345,000	142,000	10.6%	0.32	3.03
11	575,000	1,386,000	151,000	10.9%	0.41	3.81
12	550,000	1,376,000	168,000	12.2%	0.40	3.27
13	690,000	1,017,000	126,000	12.4%	0.68	5.46
14	568,000	1,183,000	157,000	13.2%	0.48	3.63
15	391,000	1,255,000	178,000	14.2%	0.31	2.20
16	520,000	1,282,000	186,000	14.5%	0.41	2.80
17	275,000	1,172,000	171,000	14.6%	0.23	1.61
18	594,000	1,315,000	203,000	15.4%	0.45	2.93
19	565,000	1,049,000	172,000	16.4%	0.54	3.29
20	577,000	1,280,000	213,000	16.6%	0.45	2.71
21	700,000	1,176,000	215,000	18.3%	0.59	3.26
22	650,000	1,050,000	210,000	20.0%	0.62	3.10
23	545,000	1,017,000	204,000	20.1%	0.54	2.67
24	700,000	1,250,000	275,000	22.0%	0.56	2.55

EXHIBIT 2.1 Addition of SDE% to Comparable Data

with the lowest level of profitability (as outlined) had an average SDE% of 5.5%, and their average revenue multiplier was only 0.21. The five most profitable companies (as outlined), had an average SDE% of 18.7% and an average revenue multiplier of 0.54.

Clearly, we can see that the level of profitability was a large factor in a company's selling price and its resulting revenue multiplier.

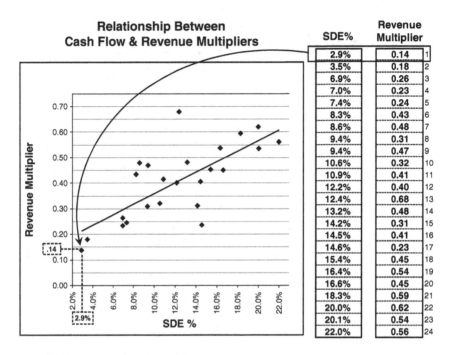

SDE%	Revenue Multiplier	
2.9%	0.14	1
3.5%	0.18	2
6.9%	0.26	3
7.0%	0.23	4
7.4%	0.24	5
8.3%	0.43	6
8.6%	0.48	7
9.4%	0.31	8
9.4%	0.47	9
10.6%	0.32	10
10.9%	0.41	11
12.2%	0.40	12
12.4%	0.68	13
13.2%	0.48	14
14.2%	0.31	15
14.5%	0.41	16
14.6%	0.23	17
15.4%	0.45	18
16.4%	0.54	19
16.6%	0.45	20
18.3%	0.59	21
20.0%	0.62	22
20.1%	0.54	23
22.0%	0.56	24

EXHIBIT 2.2 SDE% vs. Revenue Multiplier

To further dramatize the effect of the level of profitability on a company's revenue multiplier, we will plot the data from the SDE% column in Exhibit 2.1 against the data in the revenue multiplier column.

The horizontal axis (the X-axis) in Exhibit 2.2 shows the level of a company's profitability (as measured by SDE%). The farther to the right a company is positioned, the greater its level of profitability. The vertical axis (the Y-axis) shows the company's corresponding revenue multiplier; the higher a company is positioned on the vertical axis, the greater its revenue multiplier.

Each dot represents the position of each transaction in our sample given its level of profitability (SDE%) and its corresponding revenue multiplier. For example, the dot representing transaction #1 on the graph is highlighted on the chart to show its position given an SDE% of 2.9% and multiplier of 0.14.

When plotting all 24 transactions on the graph we can readily see the strong relationship between the level of a company's profitability and its revenue multiplier. The companies with greater profitability tend to be positioned farther to the right and higher up on the graph, meaning that the more profitable they are, the higher their revenue multipliers tend to be. One could easily take a ruler and draw a trend line that represents the pattern of the 24 dots that we see.

REGRESSION IS A "BEST-FITTING" TREND LINE

Or we can use regression to calculate the line with precision. In Exhibit 2.3, a regression was used to calculate the trend line. The regression line represents the "best fit" to all the

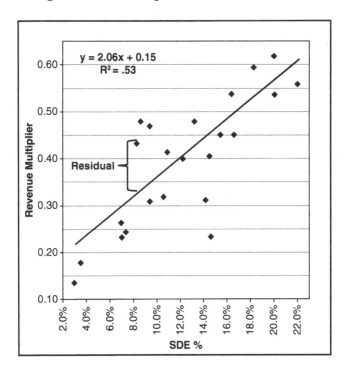

EXHIBIT 2.3 Regression of SDE% vs. Revenue Multiplier

dots identifying each of the 24 transactions in the sample. By "best fit" we mean, if one measured the vertical distance that each dot is from the trend line (Excel refers to the measure of vertical distance as the "residual," as shown in the previous graph), the combined total distance of all the dots that are above the regression line will equal the total combined distance of all the dots that are below the regression line. In other words, the total of all the dots' residuals above the trend line minus the total distance of all the dots' residuals below the line will equal zero. You cannot tweak the regression trend line any differently and get it closer to all the dots simultaneously. **Regression is nothing more than a trend line that we could have duplicated ourselves with a ruler and a pencil. It is that uncomplicated.**

But the most essential element to our regression methodology is the fact that we are using the transaction's cash flow profit margin (SDE%) as the independent variable to predict the revenue multiplier. This is where most other attempts at using regression in the Market Approach fail. They use the wrong independent variable. The SDE% is the holy grail in this methodology.

More importantly, the regression gives us the formula for the trend line. The formula is simply that of a straight line; something we all learned in algebra in high school:

$$y = mx + b$$

In this case "x" is our subject's SDE% and "y" is the revenue multiplier for the subject for which we are trying to solve. By multiplying our subject's SDE% by the "m" coefficient and adding the "b" constant we can calculate our subject's revenue multiplier that is based on its level of profitability, not some fixed constant that medians give us.

ONE PICTURE = 1,000 WORDS

Now, remember the median that we calculated for our sample in the previous chapter that was supposed to be "the measure of central tendency that shows us where the market is?"

EXHIBIT 1.1

	Price	Revenue	Cash Flow	Rev. Mult. Range	CF Mult. Range
Avg	$487,000	$1,220,000	$148,000	0.41	3.57
		Lower Quartile =		0.30	2.89
		Median =		0.42	3.30
		Upper Quartile =		0.49	4.02

We will now graph the median on the chart below to see if it does a better job at determining the appropriate revenue multiplier for our subject.

In Exhibit 2.4 the median is the dotted line. Note that it is a flat line intersecting the vertical (or Y) axis at 0.42. As we move

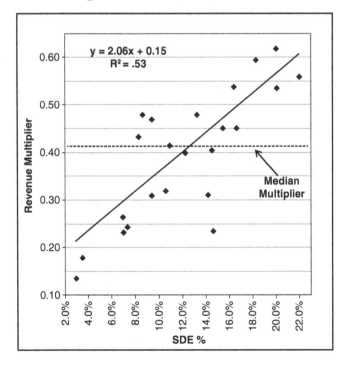

EXHIBIT 2.4 Trend Line vs. Median

from left to right on the graph, the median always stays level at 0.42. In other words, regardless of the level of profitability a company exhibits, the median revenue multiplier will always be 0.42. The dots representing the transactions in our sample and the regression trend line clearly show us that as a company becomes more profitable, its revenue multiplier tends to increase. In other words, there is a strong correlation between a company's operating profit margin and its corresponding revenue multiplier.

If an appraiser presents the above graph in his or her valuation, no jury or judge would ever consider the median multiplier as representative of "where the market is."

From the above graph we can now readily see why the results of our three examples illustrated in the prior chapter were so skewed. The unprofitable company in our second example had an SDE% that would be on the far-left side of the above graph. The median revenue multiplier of 0.42 would clearly overvalue the subject given the fact that there were more than a half dozen unprofitable transactions in our sample that only earned multipliers of 0.14 to 0.35.

The highly profitable company in our third example had an SDE% that would be on the far-right side of the above graph. Here again, the median multiplier of 0.42 would undervalue our subject given that there were at least ten comparables that earned multipliers of 0.45 to 0.68.

In fact, out of all of the 24 transactions in our sample, only one earned a multiplier of 0.42—the transaction representing the median. If the median is "where the market is," how does one explain the other 23 transactions whose multipliers were radically different from the median?

The last step in presenting compelling evidence in support of the regression methodology is to plot our subject's SDE% on the graph. In our third example from the previous chapter we calculated the subject's SDE% at 18.3% ($220,000 ÷ $1,200,000). The median revenue multiplier was 0.42; this gave us an estimated value of $504,000, which we determined was too low.

However, the median cash flow multiplier produced a value of $726,000, which we felt was too high.

Exhibit 2.5 below overlays the above subject company's SDE% onto Exhibit 2.4. We can calculate the subject's appropriate revenue multiplier manually by plotting a line that intersects the horizontal (or X) axis at 18.3% and moves vertically to the regression trend line. From there we move horizontally left and note that it intersects the Y-axis at about 0.53.

EXHIBIT 1.4a   High-Profit Subject Company

Example #3
High-Profit Subject Company:

		SDE%
Revenue	$1,200,000	SDE%
Cash Flow	$220,000	18.3%

Using Median Multiplier Values
$1,200,000 × 0.42 = $504,000
$220,000 × 3.30 = $726,000

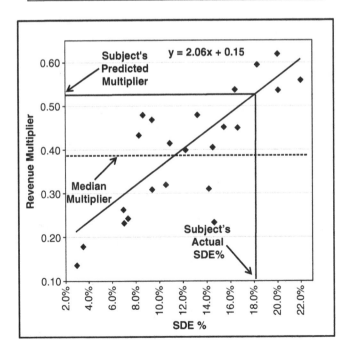

EXHIBIT 2.5   Graphing a Highly Profitable Company

More precisely, we can use the regression's formula for the trend line, which was y = 2.06x + 0.15. By inserting our subject's SDE% for the "x" factor, the resulting math is:

$$2.06 \times 18.3\% + 0.15 = 0.53$$
$$0.53 \times \$1,200,000 = \$636,000$$

Is $636,000 a reasonable value given that the median revenue multiplier value was $504,000 and the median cash flow multiplier value was $726,000? If we averaged the two median multiplier values, which most appraisers usually do, the resulting value would be $615,000. Since our subject's level of profitability was 18.3% and the entire sample only averaged 12.1% ($148,000 ÷ $1,220,000), it is, indeed, reasonable that our subject would be accorded a higher value.

However, we are not quite done with the methodology. Our sample of transactions undoubtedly had outliers that may have skewed our results. As we will demonstrate in the following chapters, the brokers who submit transactional data to the various databases often make errors that overstate company profits or the selling price of the business. It may also be the case that the company may be in a very desirable high-growth community or was the product of a strategic buyout that pushed the price of the business to extraordinarily high levels. Conversely, the business may have been in a rapidly declining neighborhood or the owner had just passed away prompting a quick sale at below-market rates.

The transactional data does not give us a hint as to why a selling price appeared too high or too low. Regardless, the standard of value for most valuations is the fair market value, in which we are looking for a selling price between a random buyer and a random seller for a business that has been exposed to the market for a reasonable amount of time. Hence, these outlier transactions do not conform to the standard of value.

An additional element with the regression methodology is that it can statistically identify outliers. Outliers are transactions whose multipliers are so much higher or lower than the majority of transactions that their values are highly suspect. By using regression to identify outliers, the appraiser can't be accused of "cherry picking" transactions for the sample. The regression's statistical analysis will identify equal numbers of inordinately high multipliers and exceedingly low multipliers. Basically, the median is doing the same thing, only it technically identifies *all* transactions above or below the median as outliers. Regression eliminates a small percentage of outliers so that the primary trend in the marketplace can be identified.

CHAPTER 3

Identifying Outliers Using Regression

There will always be a few transactions in every sample whose actual selling price was radically different from the price suggested by the regression trend line (i.e., they are significantly out of alignment with the rest of the market.) The regression analysis not only plots a line that best represents where the market is but also calculates what is referred to as standard error lines. The standard error is a statistical measurement similar to standard deviation. The difference is the standard deviation is a measure of dispersion around a single point in a sample (the mean), whereas the standard error is the same measure dispersion around the regression line. The standard error calculates the upper and lower boundaries between which most of the multipliers (68%) in a sample should fall.

Theoretically, 16% of the sample's transactions should have revenue multipliers that fall above the upper standard error line and 16% of transactions should fall below the lower standard error line. Those transactions that fall outside these boundaries are companies whose selling-price multiples were so far above or below the rest of the market that the transactional data must be considered flawed or not conforming to the stated standard of value. These "outliers," as they are referred to, will be removed from our sample of comparables.

The sample from Exhibit 2.3 produced a standard error of 0.10. Exhibit 3.1, below, adds two dotted lines to the graph that are parallel to the trend line reflecting the standard error boundaries. The upper-boundary line is 0.10 higher (on the Y-axis) than the trend line, and the lower-boundary line is 0.10 lower than the trend line.

The remaining 68% of the sample, then, are transactions that best define the market where in all probability our subject will fall. Exhibit 3.1 identified six transactions out of the sample of 24 that fell outside the standard error boundaries (see Exhibit 3.2 below). By removing those outliers, the remaining 18 transactions will generally present a visually compelling argument that the regression trend line is where the market is, not the median.

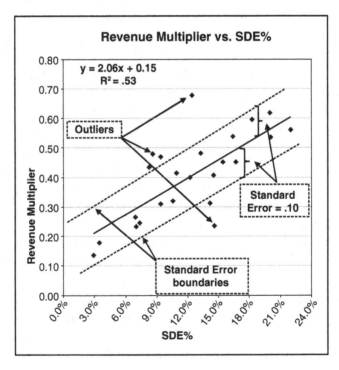

EXHIBIT 3.1   Standard Error Lines Showing Outliers

EXHIBIT 3.2 Outliers

	SDE%	Actual Multiplier	Predicted Multiplier	Residuals
1	2.9%	0.136	0.213	−0.077
2	3.5%	0.179	0.225	−0.045
3	6.9%	0.264	0.296	−0.032
4	7.0%	0.232	0.297	−0.064
5	7.4%	0.244	0.304	−0.060
6	8.3%	0.433	0.323	0.110
7	8.6%	0.479	0.330	0.149
8	9.4%	0.310	0.346	−0.036
9	9.4%	0.469	0.346	0.123
10	10.6%	0.320	0.370	−0.051
11	10.9%	0.415	0.377	0.037
12	12.2%	0.400	0.405	−0.005
13	12.4%	0.678	0.409	0.269
14	13.2%	0.480	0.426	0.054
15	14.2%	0.312	0.445	−0.134
16	14.5%	0.406	0.452	−0.046
17	14.6%	0.235	0.454	−0.219
18	15.4%	0.452	0.471	−0.019
19	16.4%	0.538	0.491	0.048
20	16.6%	0.451	0.496	−0.045
21	18.3%	0.595	0.530	0.065
22	20.0%	0.619	0.565	0.054
23	20.1%	0.536	0.566	−0.031
24	22.0%	0.560	0.606	−0.046

From Exhibit 3.3 we can see that after removing the outliers, the majority of the transactions line up fairly close to the trend line, whereas the median is a constant which is unaffected by the level of a company's profitability.

In Exhibit 3.2 the transactions that are shaded in gray are those that fell outside the standard error lines and are considered outliers. In other words, the absolute value of their residuals was greater than the standard error of 0.10.

In the following chapters you will be shown the printout from Excel's regression that identifies which transactions are outliers.

After the outliers are removed from the sample, a second regression is performed on the smaller refined sample of 18. In Exhibit 3.3 below note that the remaining 18 transactions are clustered tightly about the trend line. Once the outliers are removed, we can see that the majority of the revenue multipliers of the sample of transactions follow a very predictable pattern.

Regression provides us with a statistical measure of the "tightness" or dispersion of that pattern called R^2 (R squared). The R^2 statistic gives us a statistical measure of the accuracy of the regression that we can use to compare different samples. An R^2 ranges from 0 to 1.0. If all the transactions lined up

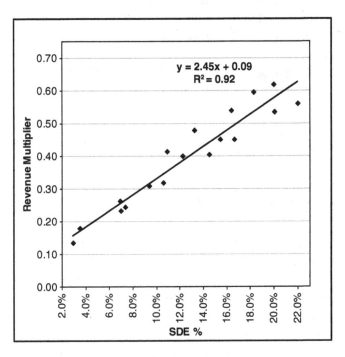

EXHIBIT 3.3   Second Regression with Outliers Removed

exactly on the regression line, then R^2 would be 1.0. If all the transactions' dots are scattered randomly throughout the graph, R^2 would be 0.0. A 0.0 would indicate that there is no correlation between a transaction's SDE% profit margin and its corresponding revenue multiplier. Interestingly, as R^2 approaches 0.0 the regression line tends to flatten out and at 0.0 the line becomes flat and is approximately the mean of the sample. In other words, if there is no correlation between profitability and the resulting revenue multiplier, the regression will give us a value that is very close to the one calculated by medians used in the conventional methodology.

In the first regression shown in Exhibit 3.1 note that R^2 was 0.53. Generally, any value greater than 0.50 is considered a good correlation between SDE% and the multiplier. However, as we will see in subsequent chapters, even in samples with an R^2 as low as 0.25 to 0.30, there still is a visible correlation between SDE% and the corresponding multiplier.

In Exhibit 3.3, the second regression with the outliers removed produced an R^2 of 0.92, a significant improvement over the first regression.

The second regression also gives us a new formula for the trend line:

$$y = 2.45x + 0.09$$

Inserting the 18.3% SDE% from the highly profitable subject company that we used in Exhibit 1.4 we have:

$$2.45 \times 0.183 + .09 = 0.54$$
$$\$1,200,000 \times 0.54 = \$648,000$$

The resulting revenue multiplier of 0.54 produces an estimated value of $648,000. Again, the median revenue multiplier for this highly profitable company suggested a value of only $504,000 while the median cash flow multiplier suggested a $726,000 value (from Exhibit 1.4a following). Even if we averaged those two values (which most appraisers typically do), the average value would be $615,000.

EXHIBIT 1.4a   High-Profit Subject Company

Example #3
High-Profit Subject Company:

High-Profit Subject Company:		
Revenue	$1,200,000	
Cash Flow	$220,000	18.3%
Using Median Multiplier Values		
$1,200,000 × 0.42 = $504,000		
$220,000 × 3.30 = $726,000		

Is $648,000 a reasonable value compared to the average median value of $615,000? Our subject's operating profit margin (SDE%) was 18.3%, which is moderately higher than the median of our sample of 12.3%. Given that it is considerably more profitable than most of the 24 transactions in our sample, the higher value of $648,000 is indeed reasonable.

CHAPTER 4

Cash Flow Multiplier Regression

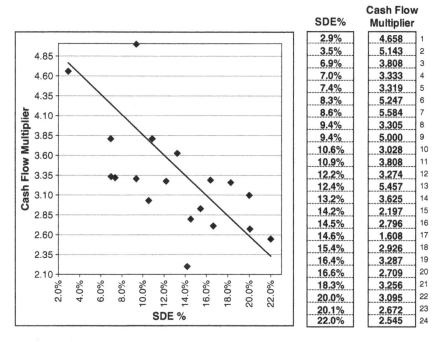

SDE%	Cash Flow Multiplier	
2.9%	4.658	1
3.5%	5.143	2
6.9%	3.808	3
7.0%	3.333	4
7.4%	3.319	5
8.3%	5.247	6
8.6%	5.584	7
9.4%	3.305	8
9.4%	5.000	9
10.6%	3.028	10
10.9%	3.808	11
12.2%	3.274	12
12.4%	5.457	13
13.2%	3.625	14
14.2%	2.197	15
14.5%	2.796	16
14.6%	1.608	17
15.4%	2.926	18
16.4%	3.287	19
16.6%	2.709	20
18.3%	3.256	21
20.0%	3.095	22
20.1%	2.672	23
22.0%	2.545	24

EXHIBIT 4.1 SDE% vs. Cash Flow Multipliers

The logic surrounding the use of regression to predict revenue multipliers makes perfect sense—the higher a company's level of profitability, the higher its revenue multiplier will likely be. However, this logic is completely the opposite when calculating cash flow multipliers. If we go back to Exhibit 2.1 and retrieve the SDE% and cash flow multipliers for each of our 24 transactions, the graph will look like Exhibit 4.1. Amazingly, there is an inverted relationship between a company's level of profitability and its cash flow multiplier!

As we move to the right on the X-axis, the cash flow profit margins increase. However, we notice that as we moved right, the dots representing the transactions move lower and lower on the chart, indicating a smaller cash flow multiplier.

In other words, the greater the level of a company's profitability, the lower its cash flow multiplier.

This is just counterintuitive. After all, we have always been taught that the more profitable companies have a tendency to sell for higher prices. That axiom is still true. But when an appraiser determines the appropriate cash flow multiplier for the subject company, he is not using the actual cash flow from the sample's transaction in his calculations. He is using a ratio. That ratio is the selling price ÷ SDE—the cash flow multiplier. Since we are dealing with a ratio, we bring into the process that little foible of ratios—the smaller the denominator, the larger the resulting number.

Observe from Exhibit 4.2:

From our original table of 24 comparables we note that the upper five transactions had an average cash flow of $70,000 and an average selling price of $270,000. The five highly profitable transactions had an average cash flow of $215,000 and an average selling price of $607,000.

Clearly companies with higher cash flow sold for higher prices. The five high-profit transactions had over three times the level of cash flow than the five low-profit transactions and as a result they sold for an average of 225% more.

However, the cash flow multiplier ratio for the least profitable transaction was 4.66, whereas for the most profitable transaction it was 2.55. In the case of the least profitable transaction, the selling price was a very small $170,000. However,

	Selling Price (b)		Cash Flow (SDE) (d)		Cash Flow Multiplier (b) ÷ (d)
1	170,000		37,000		4.66
2	252,000		49,000		5.14
3	315,000		83,000		3.81
4	300,000		90,000		3.33
5	312,000		94,000		3.32
6	509,000		97,000		5.25
7	575,000		115,000		5.00
8	575,000		103,000		5.58
9	347,000		105,000		3.30
10	430,000		142,000		3.03
11	575,000		151,000		3.81
12	550,000		168,000		3.27
13	690,000		126,000		5.46
14	568,000		157,000		3.63
15	391,000		178,000		2.20
16	520,000		186,000		2.80
17	275,000		171,000		1.61
18	594,000		203,000		2.93
19	700,000		215,000		3.26
20	565,000		172,000		3.29
21	577,000		213,000		2.71
22	650,000		210,000		3.10
23	545,000		204,000		2.67
24	700,000		275,000		2.55

EXHIBIT 4.2 Increasing Cash Flow and Selling Price

its cash flow (the denominator in the ratio) was an even smaller $37,000. Hence, the small denominator in the cash flow multiplier ratio produced a logic-defying 4.66 multiplier compared to the most profitable company's 2.55.

This is precisely why every appraiser using conventional methodology ends up with values from the cash flow and revenue multipliers that are often wildly divergent. In Chapter 1 when we were trying to value the highly profitable company, the suggestion was that highly profitable companies should be accorded the upper quartile multipliers. The upper-quartile revenue multiplier of 0.49 was indeed representative of highly profitable companies. However, the upper quartile of cash flow multipliers was a collection of transactions with the highest multipliers, which we now know represented the least profitable companies.

EXHIBIT 1.1b

	Price	Revenue	Cash Flow	Rev. Mult. Range	CF Mult. Range
Avg	$487,000	$1,220,000	$148,000	0.41	3.57
	Lower Quartile =			0.30	2.89
	Median =			0.42	3.30
	Upper Quartile =			0.49	4.02

Consequently, when valuing a highly profitable company, the conventional methodology used by every appraiser today aligns the revenue multipliers of the most profitable companies with the subject company and then unwittingly aligns the cash flow multipliers for the least profitable companies with the subject.

The second reason that cash flow multipliers decrease as companies become more profitable is that there is a decreasing return to value as cash flow increases. Companies of similar size and in similar industries typically generate more value for their first $50,000 in cash flow than they do for their last $50,000. In other words, as companies increase in profitability, their cash flow increases at a faster rate than the corresponding selling prices of businesses. For example, in Exhibit 4.2 we find the five least profitable transactions had selling prices averaging $270,000 and cash flow averaging $70,000. The five most profitable transactions had an average selling price of $634,000 and cash flow averaging $223,000. Moving from the lowest profitable companies to the highest we find that their average selling prices increased by 2.3 ($634,000 / $270,000). However, their cash flow increased by 3.07 ($215,000 / $70,000). Since cash flow increases at a faster rate than selling price, the corresponding cash flow multipliers (selling price / cash flow) tend to decrease.

Conventional Market Approach methodologies do not capture the inverted relationship between a company's cash flow multiplier and its level of profitability. As we saw with the revenue multipliers, the median of the sample of transactions is a flat line on the graph, which indicates that regardless of the subject's level of profitability, the median multiplier would always be the appraiser's choice in valuing the subject business. This inverted relationship causes median cash flow multiplier values to dive significantly below the median revenue multiplier values in underperforming companies and, conversely, rise well above the median revenue multiplier values in high-performing companies.

In Exhibit 4.3 note that the regression equation has a negative "x" coefficient, indicating a downward-sloping trend line. This first regression only produced an R^2 of 0.37. However, even though this measure of dispersion is below our comfort level of 0.50 we can still visually observe a definite correlation between the transactions' SDE% and their corresponding cash flow multipliers.

The initial regression gave us the following equation:

$$y = -12.77x + 5.13$$

Applying the 18.3% SDE% from our highly-profitable company in our initial Example 3 we arrive at the value:

$$-12.77 \times 0.183 + 5.13 = 2.79$$

$$2.79 \times \$220,000 = \$613,800$$

The median multiplier of 3.30, suggesting a value of $726,000, clearly overpriced the business. The median ignored

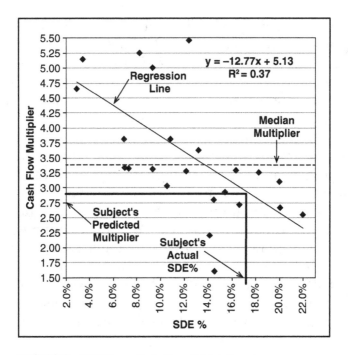

EXHIBIT 4.3　SDE% vs. Cash Flow Multipliers

the fact that ten transactions at the subject's level of profitability had multipliers much lower, ranging from 1.6 to 3.1.

Exhibit 4.3 is the first regression that included all 24 of the sample's transactions. The regression also gave us a standard error of 0.87, which we will use to identify outlying transactions. Exhibit 4.4 shows the actual multiplier of each of the 24 transactions in the sample. Using the above regression formula, each transaction's predicted multiplier and the residual difference is calculated. Those transactions where the absolute value of the residual is greater than the 0.87 standard error will be considered outliers. The outliers are shaded in gray.

Earlier in the book we noted that the regression line was a "best fit" to all the transactions in a sample. We noted that the total residuals above the regression line minus the total residuals below the regression line would equal zero. If one totals the 24

EXHIBIT 4.4 Outliers Identified

	SDE%	Actual Multiplier	Predicted Multiplier	Residual
1	2.9%	4.658	4.765	−0.107
2	3.5%	5.143	4.692	0.450
3	6.9%	3.808	4.252	−0.444
4	7.0%	3.333	4.247	−0.915
5	7.4%	3.319	4.199	−0.879
6	8.3%	5.247	4.084	1.164
7	8.6%	5.584	4.042	1.542
8	9.4%	3.305	3.941	−0.636
9	9.4%	5.000	3.939	1.061
10	10.6%	3.028	3.790	−0.762
11	10.9%	3.808	3.747	0.061
12	12.2%	3.274	3.579	−0.305
13	12.4%	5.457	3.551	1.906
14	13.2%	3.625	3.446	0.179
15	14.2%	2.197	3.327	−1.130
16	14.5%	2.796	3.285	−0.490
17	14.6%	1.608	3.274	−1.666
18	15.4%	2.926	3.167	−0.241
19	16.4%	3.287	3.046	0.241
20	16.6%	2.709	3.013	−0.304
21	18.3%	3.256	2.804	0.451
22	20.0%	3.095	2.584	0.511
23	20.1%	2.672	2.577	0.095
24	22.0%	2.545	2.329	0.217

values in the "Residual" column in Exhibit 4.4 above, it will equal zero, thus, conforming to our definition of "best fit."

The eight outliers identified in the above table are then removed from the sample and a second regression is run on the smaller sample of 16 transactions.

The second regression produced a much-improved R^2 increasing from 0.37 to 0.63 and gave us a second regression equation to calculate the subject's value.

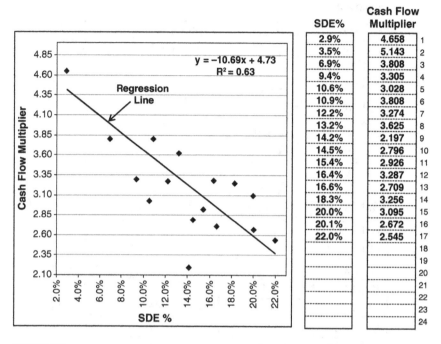

	SDE%	Cash Flow Multiplier	
	2.9%	4.658	1
	3.5%	5.143	2
	6.9%	3.808	3
	9.4%	3.305	4
	10.6%	3.028	5
	10.9%	3.808	6
	12.2%	3.274	7
	13.2%	3.625	8
	14.2%	2.197	9
	14.5%	2.796	10
	15.4%	2.926	11
	16.4%	3.287	12
	16.6%	2.709	13
	18.3%	3.256	14
	20.0%	3.095	15
	20.1%	2.672	16
	22.0%	2.545	17
			18
			19
			20
			21
			22
			23
			24

EXHIBIT 4.5 Regression with Outliers Removed

Applying the 18.3% SDE% from our highly profitable company to the new regression equation we arrive at the value:

$$-10.69 \times 0.183 + 4.73 = 2.77$$

$$2.77 \times \$220,000 = \$609,400$$

EXHIBIT 1.4a A High-Profit Subject Company

Example #3
High-Profit Subject Company:
Revenue $1,200,000 SDE%
Cash Flow $220,000 18.3%
Using Median Multiplier Values
$1,200,000 × 0.42 = $504,000
$220,000 × 3.30 = $726,000

The resulting cash flow multiplier of 2.77 produces an estimated value of $609,400. From Exhibit 4.6 we noted that the median cash flow multiplier for this highly profitable company suggested a value of only $504,000, and the median cash flow multiplier suggested a $726,000 value. The values produced by the two median multipliers were $222,000 apart. Even if an appraiser selected the $615,000 average of those two values, the spread between the two median values is so great that it begs to be challenged.

It is important to note that the value that we calculated using the regression's revenue multiplier was $648,000, just a $38,600 difference from the value calculated by the cash flow regression. The regression methodology will always produce values that are fairly close, such that an average would appear reasonable.

To further demonstrate, we calculated the values of all three of the examples that we analyzed in the first chapter using the same regression formulas.

Revenue Multiplier formula: $y = 2.45x + .09$

Cash Flow Multiplier formula: $y = -10.69x + 4.73$

EXHIBIT 4.6   Average Subject Company

Example #1
Average Subject Company:
Revenue $1,200,000 SDE%
Cash Flow $150,000 12.50%
Using Regression Multipliers
$1,200,000 × .40 = $480,000
$150,000 × 3.39 = $508,500
Average = $494,250
Difference = $28,500
Using Median Multiplier Values
$1,200,000 × .42 = $504,000
$150,000 × 3.30 = $495,000
Average = $499,500
Difference = $9,000

From the three examples here we can see that for companies that are at the opposite ends of the profitability spectrum, the regression methodology produces far more reasonable and defensible values than the median multipliers produce.

In Example #1, the two regression values were $28,500 apart. Even though it was a larger spread than the median values, it was still quite small. As such, an appraiser would not be challenged had he or she opined value of $494,250, the average of the two multiplier values, or rounded the final value to $500,000.

In Example #2, the regression values were just $24,500 apart, whereas the median values were $223,500 apart and

EXHIBIT 4.7   Low-Profit Subject Company

Example #2
Low-Profit Subject Company:
Revenue $1,200,000 SDE%
Cash Flow $85,000 7.1%
Using Regression Multipliers
$1,200,000 × .264 = $316,800
$85,000 × 3.971 = $337,535
Average = $327,168
Difference = $20,735
Using Median Multiplier Values
$1,200,000 × .42 = $504,000
$85,000 × 3.30 = $280,500
Average = $392,250
Difference = $223,500
Using Lower Quartile Multiplier Values
$1,200,000 × .30 = $360,000
$85,000 × 2.89 = $245,650
Average = $302,825
Difference = $114,350

EXHIBIT 4.8   High-Profit Subject Company

Example #3
High-Profit Subject Company:
Revenue $1,200,000 SDE%
Cash Flow $220,000 18.3%
<u>Using Regression Multipliers</u>
$1,200,000 × .54 = $648,000
$220,000 × 2.77 = $609,400
Average = $628,700
Difference = $38,600
<u>Using Median Multiplier Values</u>
$1,200,000 × .42 = $504,000
$220,000 × 3.30 = $726,000
Average = $615,000
Difference = $222,000
<u>Using Upper Quartile Multiplier Values</u>
$1,200,000 × .49 = $588,000
$220,000 × 4.02 = $884,400
Average = $736,200
Difference = $296,400

the lower quartile values were $114,350 apart. The average value of the two medians and the two lower quartile values was $347,000, slightly higher than the regression's $327,000. However, the subject's 7.1% profit margin was below the 8.5% lower quartile margin. Hence, the lower value is reasonable.

In Example #3, the regression values were only $38,600 apart, whereas the median values were $222,000 apart and the upper quartile values were $296,400 apart. The average of the two median values and the two upper quartile values was $675,000, which was modestly higher than the $629,000 regression average. However, the upper quartile value was clearly way out of line, thus, skewing the results.

CHAPTER 5

Enterprise Multiplier

The enterprise multipliers are subsets of the standard revenue and cash flow multipliers that we studied previously. (As a side bar, the methodology is also the way that Bizcomps calculates these two multipliers.) The enterprise revenue multiplier is the selling price less inventory divided by revenue, and the enterprise cash flow multiplier is the selling price less inventory divided by cash flow. Inventory is generally the most volatile asset on a company's balance sheet. Hence, removing it before calculating the multipliers makes the resulting ratio much more stable and predictable.

When small inventory-carrying businesses are sold, the selling price is usually listed at a fixed base price plus an unknown inventory value to be determined at a later date. A physical inventory is usually taken around the day escrow closes, and the full amount is added to the base selling price. Inventory fluctuates up and down significantly from day to day due to sales and stock replenishment. Hence, the final selling price of a business fluctuates up and down by the same amount. Consequently, by removing inventory from the selling price, the resulting value is far more stable, and comparing one business to the next is far more meaningful.

The enterprise methodology is particularly useful for predicting the values of companies that derive most of their revenue from the sale of inventory—retailers, wholesalers,

EXHIBIT 5.1 Enterprise Multipliers

	Selling Price	Revenue (b)	Cash Flow (c)	Inventory (d)	SDE% (c) ÷ (b)	Revenue Multiplier	Cash Flow Multiplier	Enterprise Multiplier
				ABC Machine Shop				
1	450,000	2,971,358	233,651	100,000	7.9%	0.15	1.93	0.12
2	940,000	3,705,000	404,000	40,000	10.9%	0.25	2.33	0.24
3	990,000	3,500,000	427,841	187,510	12.2%	0.28	2.31	0.23
4	530,183	1,801,092	254,321	50,000	14.1%	0.29	2.08	0.27
5	766,959	2,233,258	331,424	361,630	14.8%	0.34	2.31	0.18
6	1,395,000	2,930,376	496,820	40,947	17.0%	0.48	2.81	0.46
7	2,208,692	3,620,708	667,675	269,471	18.4%	0.61	3.31	0.54
8	1,510,022	2,386,283	458,137	110,022	19.2%	0.63	3.30	0.59
9	1,300,000	1,900,000	385,000	183,501	20.3%	0.68	3.38	0.59
10	1,566,925	2,801,382	668,522	512,393	23.9%	0.56	2.34	0.38
11	925,000	1,528,734	372,403	38,490	24.4%	0.61	2.48	0.58
12	3,500,000	3,404,875	881,344	123,000	25.9%	1.03	3.97	0.99
13	1,700,000	2,533,000	693,000	126,000	27.4%	0.67	2.45	0.62
14	1,150,000	1,720,000	480,000	30,000	27.9%	0.67	2.40	0.65
15	2,600,000	2,900,000	814,000	550,504	28.1%	0.90	3.19	0.71
16	1,700,000	1,960,000	552,000	233,964	28.2%	0.87	3.08	0.75
17	2,060,833	3,185,280	901,411	540,003	28.3%	0.65	2.29	0.48
18	3,520,000	2,813,127	821,340	81,593	29.2%	1.25	4.29	1.22
19	1,100,000	1,503,000	440,000	75,000	29.3%	0.73	2.50	0.68
20	4,250,000	3,989,222	1,196,766	349,212	30.0%	1.07	3.55	0.98
21	1,770,000	2,000,000	650,000	20,000	32.5%	0.89	2.72	0.88
22	3,530,000	3,201,897	1,080,121	274,581	33.7%	1.10	3.27	1.02
23	1,160,000	1,502,594	562,269	75,000	37.4%	0.77	2.06	0.72
24	1,766,244	2,612,660	598,785	190,123	SDE % Range	Revenue Mult	Cash Flow Mult	Enterprise Mult
Lower Quartile					17.7%	0.52	2.32	0.42
Median					25.9%	0.67	2.50	0.59
Upper Quartile					28.8%	0.88	3.29	0.74
Average					23.5%	0.67	2.80	0.60

and manufacturers. Since service-type companies do not carry inventory, their revenue multiplier would technically be the same as their enterprise revenue multiplier. ([selling price ÷ revenue] is the same as [(selling price − $0 inventory) ÷ revenue]). Hence, using enterprise multipliers for these companies does not contribute anything toward the conclusion of value and should not be used.

It has also been my experience after analyzing several thousand samples that the enterprise revenue multipliers often produced as good or better R^2 ratings than the standard revenue multipliers. Enterprise cash flow multipliers, however, produced worse R^2 ratings than their counterparts. As a result, enterprise cash flow multipliers generally contributed little to the final conclusion of value. Hence, going forward we will only include the enterprise revenue multiplier in our analysis (which I shall abbreviate as enterprise multipliers).

When building a sample to include the enterprise multipliers, we must add two new columns of data to the tables that were used in earlier chapters—inventory and the enterprise multiplier. (See Exhibit 5.1.) With the addition of the inventory value we can calculate the median enterprise multipliers.

From Exhibit 5.2 we note that after running the second revenue multiplier regression with outliers removed, R^2 was a respectable 0.88. The second regression of the enterprise multipliers produced an even better R^2 of 0.90 (Exhibit 5.3).

Assuming that our subject company generated $2,292,000 in revenue, $600,000 in SDE, and $130,000 in inventory, the three multipliers would yield the following values:

Revenue Multiplier

$$\$2,292,000 \times 0.67 = \underline{\underline{\$1,536,000}}$$

Cash Flow Multiplier

$$\$600,000 \times 2.50 = \underline{\underline{\$1,500,000}}$$

Enterprise Multiplier

$$\$2,292,000 \times 0.61 + \$130,000 = \underline{\underline{\$1,528,000}}$$

The subject's average value for the three multipliers is $1,521,333.

The usefulness of the enterprise methodology becomes apparent when the subject has a much higher level of inventory than the average transaction. Assume the subject in

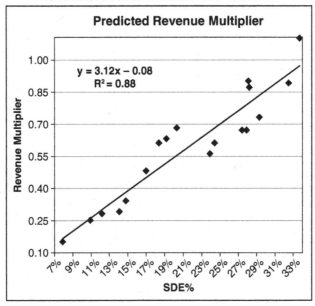

R Sq. = 0.88

Regression Formula = 3.12 × SDE% + –0.08

Subject's SDE% = 24.0%

Predicted Multiplier = **0.67**

EXHIBIT 5.2   Revenue Multiplier

the above example had $400,000 in inventory. The average transaction in the sample carried only $190,123 in inventory. The new enterprise regression value for the subject would then be: $2,292,000 × 0.61 + $400,000 = $1,798,120. The average of the three regression multiplier values is $1,611,337 [($1,536,000 + $1,500,000+ $1798,120) ÷ 3], nearly $74,000 higher than the company that only had $130,000 in inventory.

Is this a reasonable value? The top five transactions in the sample averaged $463,000 in inventory. They earned an average revenue multiplier of 0.70, an average cash flow

ENTERPRISE MULTIPLIER
FINAL REGRESSION WITH OUTLIERS REMOVED

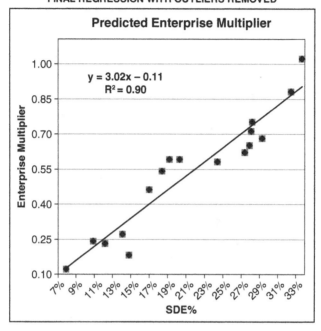

R Sq. = 0.90

Regression Formula = 3.02 × SDE% + −0.11

Subject's SDE% = 24.0%

Predicted Multiplier = 0.61

EXHIBIT 5.3   Enterprise Multiplier

multiplier of 2.69, and an average enterprise multiplier of 0.55. If we applied those multipliers to the subject with $400,000 in inventory, its value would be

$2,292,000 × .70 =	$1,604,400
$600,000 × 2.69	$1,614,000
$2,292,000 × .55 + $400,000 =	$1,660,000
Average =	$1,626,000

Hence, for a company with excess inventory, the average of the three multipliers generated by the regressions produced a value that aligns with the average values exhibited by the largest inventory-carrying companies in the whole sample.

In the above example, the subject's $400,000 in inventory represented an excess of $210,000 over the average level carried by the transactions in the sample. Consequently, the $74,000 increased value accorded to the subject only represented 35¢ on the dollar for that excess inventory. This often occurs even though the inventory is worth all of $400,000.

The offer price for the company with average inventory might take the form: $1,330,000 + $190,000 = $1,520,000. For the company with excess inventory, however, the offer price might look like: $1,194,000 + $400,000 = $1,594,000. The second company's offer price was only $74,000 higher even though there was $400,000 in inventory. The enterprise value of the business (the value net of inventory) takes the hit.

It has been my experience as a business broker that buyers often aggressively discount the value of excess inventory or fixtures and equipment when making an offer for a business. Given two companies with the same level of revenue and cash flow, the company with an average level of inventory would be the buyer's preferred choice. Or, conversely, the buyer would be reluctant to pay much more for the company with the excess inventory.

There are two reasons for this. Firstly, the buyer must borrow more money to acquire a business with excess inventory. As such, his debt service will be higher and his net cash flow will be lower than for a company with an average level of inventory. Hence, there is a negative incentive to buy a company with excess inventory.

Secondly, banks are reluctant to advance dollar for dollar for excess inventory. SBA lenders are required by the Small Business Administration to take enough collateral to secure the proposed indebtedness. In other words, a million-dollar loan ideally must have at least one million dollars in collateral securing the debt. The Small Business Administration's policy manual limits the value ascribed to the collateral being taken. For example, depending on the type of company being financed, the SBA lenders might only be allowed to give a collateral value of 50% to 85% for the inventory being financed. Consequently, a company with $500,000 in inventory may only receive credit for $350,000 in collateral value. The bank must then seek other forms of collateral to make up the $150,000 shortfall. Unfortunately for the buyer, that usually is his or her personal residence. Faced with that reality, the buyer tries to renegotiate his offer to a lower price to avoid giving up the house as collateral.

CHAPTER 6

Polynomial Regressions

In probably one out of twenty regressions performed on samples of comparables, the linear regression methodologies reviewed in the previous chapters will appear to produce unreasonable results. This occurs most frequently when the subject company itself is an outlier. That is, the subject's operating profit margin (SDE%) was well above or was below most of, or all of, the transactions in the sample. This is not to say that medians will be the better choice of metrics here because medians fail under these circumstances as well. Exhibit 6.1 is a classic example. To illustrate, the subject's SDE% in this example is 21.5%, well above almost all of the transactions in the sample.

The intersection on the regression line at an SDE% of 21.5% suggests that a cash flow multiplier of approximately 3.25 is appropriate. However, we observe that there are five highly profitable transactions in the sample that have multipliers between 3.4 and 3.6. Clearly the linear regression appears to undervalue the subject as the regression line was not responsive to those highly profitable transactions.

The same situation appears at the low-profit end of the SDE% spectrum. If our subject's SDE% was in the 2% to 4% range, the regression line does not seem to recognize the fact that two comparables in that level of profitability produced multipliers in the 4.4 to 4.5 range, well above the regression line.

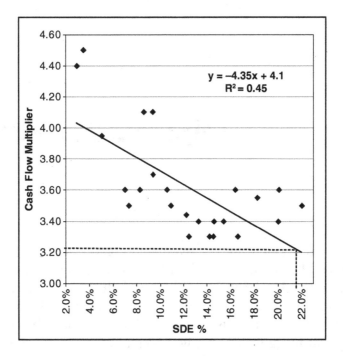

EXHIBIT 6.1   Linear Regressions on Subject's That Are Outliers

When a visual inspection of the regression graph makes us suspicious that the linear regression line is not properly recognizing either end of the SDE% spectrum, a polynomial curved regression may be the answer. By merely right-clicking on the regression line on the graph in your Excel worksheet, the Trendline Option window to the left pops up (See Exhibit 6.2). By selecting the Polynomial radio button and Order = 2, the chart will automatically recalculate a curved regression line. It will also give us a new formula and R^2.

The curved regression line in Exhibit 6.3 greatly increased the R^2 from 0.45 to 0.71, suggesting that it is the better regression. The line now appears to be influenced by the five highly profitable transactions in the sample. We also note that the curved regression is similarly influenced by several of the low profit comparables in the sample, suggesting that a subject

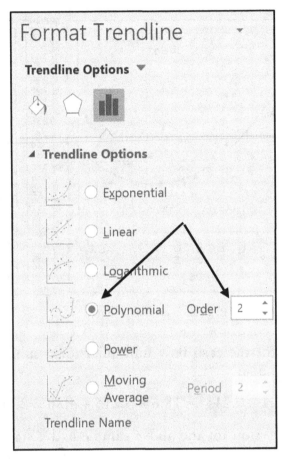

EXHIBIT 6.2 Trendline Options
Source: Used with permission from Microsoft Corporation

with a 3% or 4% SDE% should earn a cash flow multiple in the 4.2 to 4.4 range.

The polynomial curve introduces a second variable—x^2—in the regression equation making it a quadratic equation. From algebra II we remember quadratic equations take the form:

$$Y = ax^2 + mx + b$$

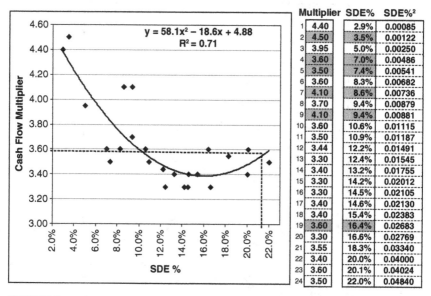

EXHIBIT 6.3   Polynomial Regression on Outlier Subject

Solving for the cash flow multiplier for a subject with an SDE% of 21.5%:

$$58.1 \times 0.215^2 - 18.6 \times 0.215 + 4.88 = 3.56$$

The regression for the above sample had a standard error of 0.191, making the transactions (shaded in gray) outliers. As in our prior regression methodologies, we will remove the outliers and perform a second regression. Note the 18 remaining transactions out of the 24 in the sample are tightly clustered about the regression line, and the R^2 increased to 0.79. The new regression formula gives us a multiplier value of 3.70. The median of the sample was 3.53. Since the subject in this example is one of the most profitable transactions, a 3.70 multiplier is clearly warranted.

As I mentioned in the beginning of this chapter, I have only found polynomial regressions to be relevant in about one out of twenty appraisals. Just because a subject has a much higher or lower level of profitability than the transactions in one's sample does not automatically mean the polynomial regression is

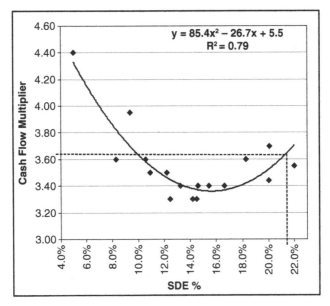

EXHIBIT 6.4 Polynomial Regressions with Outliers Removed

the better methodology. Also, a higher R^2 compared to a linear regression does not necessarily mean the polynomial regression is the better methodology. When dealing with subjects that are themselves outliers, the appraiser is cautioned to use his or her best judgment in deciding whether polynomial regressions produce a more relevant value than linear regressions.

ADDING A SECOND INDEPENDENT VARIABLE

In the previous regression methodologies, we used the SDE% of the transactions in the sample as the single independent variable used to predict the subject's multipliers. To produce a polynomial curve using Excel's regression utility, we must add a second independent variable to predict the multipliers. That second variable is the square of the SDE% for each transaction in the sample.

The addition of the SDE%^{2} variable in the regression creates the quadratic equation. The right-hand column in Exhibit 6.5 is the square of each transaction's SDE%.

EXHIBIT 6.5   Polynomial Variable

	Multiplier	SDE%	SDE%^{2}
1	4.40	2.9%	0.00085
2	4.50	3.5%	0.00122
3	3.95	5.0%	0.00250
4	3.60	7.0%	0.00486
5	3.50	7.4%	0.00541
6	3.60	8.3%	0.00682
7	4.10	8.6%	0.00736
8	3.70	9.4%	0.00879
9	4.10	9.4%	0.00881
10	3.60	10.6%	0.01115
11	3.50	10.9%	0.01187
12	3.44	12.2%	0.01491
13	3.30	12.4%	0.01545
14	3.40	13.2%	0.01755
15	3.30	14.2%	0.02012
16	3.30	14.5%	0.02105
17	3.40	14.6%	0.02130
18	3.40	15.4%	0.02383
19	3.60	16.4%	0.02683
20	3.30	16.6%	0.02769
21	3.55	18.3%	0.03340
22	3.40	20.0%	0.04000
23	3.60	20.1%	0.04024
24	3.50	22.0%	0.04840

In Chapter 10 we will learn how to use Excel's regression with two independent variables. We will also learn how to manually recreate the graphs and trendlines that are shown throughout this book. It is not necessary for the reader to learn how to use Excel's regression utility, but it does help one understand how the information is created. Regardless, in Chapter 11 the template that came with this book will be examined. It creates all the regressions and graphs automatically with just the click of one button.

CHAPTER **7**

Multiple Variable Regression

The fourth regression methodology we will employ in the Market Approach is a multiple variable regression. In the first two methodologies we studied we used a single variable, the SDE% of the transactions in the sample, to predict the multipliers of the subject. In the third methodology we used two variables, the SDE% and the square of the SDE%, to predict the multipliers of the subject. In this fourth methodology we will use four variables to predict the actual selling price of the subject: each transaction's revenue, SDE, inventory value, and fixtures and equipment value (throughout the book we will use the acronym FF&E in reference to the company's total furniture, fixture, equipment, and tenant improvements). The resulting formula will take the form:

$$SP = aRev + bSDE + cInv + dFF\&E + e$$

The advantage of this methodology is that the subject's inventory value and fixtures and equipment value (its hard assets) are now brought into the final calculation of its worth. Revenue multipliers and cash flow multipliers completely ignore the value of a company's assets. For companies that are heavily invested in inventory or fixtures, the addition of these two variables in a regression equation may produce a more relevant conclusion of value. We are also using actual values for the variables rather than ratios in the calculations, which we learned earlier could produce undesirable outcomes.

It is reasonable to conclude that companies with a higher investment in hard assets than the average transactions in the sample should earn higher selling prices. In reality this may not always be the case. However, as a business broker, I found that companies with much higher levels of hard assets than the average company often received as little as 10¢ to 25¢ on the dollar for those excess assets. The larger the excess investment, the smaller the percentage of cost the seller typically received. Regardless, the seller generally did receive some additional consideration for the excess assets.

For demonstration purposes a simplified regression analysis is graphed in Exhibit 7.1. The values for the selling prices and the gross revenues of 23 transactions were plotted on the chart, and a regression line was then calculated. The subject company's gross revenue of $2,900,000 is then located on the X-axis. By moving vertically from that point and intersecting the regression trend line we can then identify the probable selling price of $1,900,000 from the Y-axis on the left side of the chart.

The chart in Exhibit 7.1 is a single-variable regression analysis that regressed revenues against the selling price. A four-variable multiple regression is literally four of these charts layered one on top of the other with each layer representing one of the four variables. The calculated trend line then cuts through all four layers. The multiple regression formula is actually several pages long. However, an Excel spreadsheet can perform a multiple regression analysis with a few clicks of a button.

Exhibit 7.2 illustrates a sample of 23 transactions. The databases that were used provided us with the revenue, cash flow, inventory, and fixtures and equipment values.

It is important to note that when working with multiple variable regressions the columns representing the four independent variables must be side-by-side. There can be no blank columns

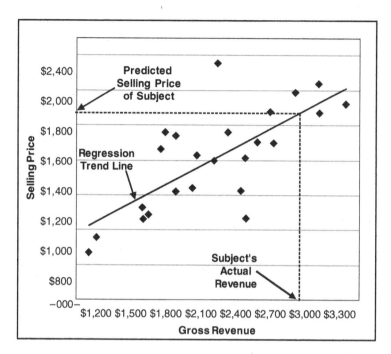

EXHIBIT 7.1 Regression of Revenue vs. Selling Price

between the four columns of variables. In addition, no individual cells can be blank (i.e., have no value). Any blank columns or cells will create an error message when running the regression utility.

The multiple regression performed on the sample below produced the following equation:

$$\text{Selling Price} = 0.102 \times \text{Rev} + 3.93 \times \text{SDE} - 1.19 \times \text{Inv}$$

$$+ 0.33 \times \text{FF\&E} + 738,640$$

By applying the above formula to each of the transactions in the sample, we can determine how closely the regression's predicted value was to the transaction's actual value.

The standard error of the regression was $363,055. Those transactions shaded in gray had residuals in which the absolute value was greater than the standard error and are, therefore, considered outliers. (See Exhibit 7.3.)

EXHIBIT 7.2   Sample of Transactions for Multiple Variable Regression

	Selling Price	Revenue	Cash Flow	Inventory	Fixtures	Rev	CF
1	450,000	2,971,358	233,651	100,000	100,000	0.15	1.93
2	940,000	3,705,000	404,000	40,000	309,000	0.25	2.33
3	990,000	3,500,000	427,841	187,510	212,489	0.28	2.31
4	530,183	1,801,092	254,321	50,000	350,000	0.29	2.08
5	766,959	2,233,258	331,424	361,630	426,657	0.34	2.31
6	1,395,000	2,930,376	496,820	40,947	48,310	0.48	2.81
7	2,208,692	3,620,708	667,675	269,471	317,928	0.61	3.31
8	1,510,022	2,386,283	458,137	110,022	600,000	0.63	3.30
9	1,300,000	1,900,000	385,000	183,501	216,498	0.68	3.38
10	1,566,925	2,801,382	668,522	512,393	604,531	0.56	2.34
11	925,000	1,528,734	372,403	38,490	45,412	0.61	2.48
12	3,500,000	3,404,875	881,344	123,000	969,482	1.03	3.97
13	1,700,000	2,533,000	693,000	126,000	50,000	0.67	2.45
14	1,150,000	1,720,000	480,000	30,000	314,000	0.67	2.40
15	2,600,000	2,900,000	814,000	550,504	649,495	0.90	3.19
16	1,700,000	1,960,000	552,000	233,964	276,035	0.87	3.08
17	2,060,833	3,185,280	901,411	540,003	637,106	0.65	2.29
18	3,520,000	2,813,127	821,340	81,593	92,462	1.25	4.29
19	1,100,000	1,503,000	440,000	75,000	68,000	0.73	2.50
20	4,250,000	3,989,222	1,196,766	349,212	412,007	1.07	3.55
21	1,770,000	2,000,000	650,000	20,000	450,000	0.89	2.72
22	3,530,000	3,201,897	1,080,121	274,581	323,956	1.10	3.27
23	1,160,000	1,502,594	562,269	75,000	68,690	0.77	2.06
Avg =	1,766,244	2,612,660	598,785	190,123	327,916	0.67	2.80

It is also noteworthy that the column of residuals in the exhibit totals to zero, thus conforming to our "best fit" definition.

This first regression produced a credible R^2 of 0.90. However, if we remove the six outliers shaded in gray and run a second regression, R^2 increases to 0.98. The R^2 generated on multiple regressions is usually higher than on single-variable regressions.

EXHIBIT 7.3 Selling Prices of Sample

	Actual	Predicted	Residuals
1	450,000	398,034	51,966
2	940,000	1,284,500	−344,500
3	990,000	1,149,029	−159,029
4	530,183	502,995	27,188
5	766,959	504,089	262,870
6	1,395,000	1,482,253	−87,253
7	2,208,692	2,042,162	166,530
8	1,510,022	1,376,383	133,639
9	1,300,000	823,186	476,814
10	1,566,925	1,767,602	−200,677
11	925,000	851,630	73,370
12	3,500,000	3,253,102	246,898
13	1,700,000	2,112,392	−412,392
14	1,150,000	1,394,277	−244,277
15	2,600,000	2,319,457	280,543
16	1,700,000	1,445,880	254,120
17	2,060,833	2,700,831	−639,998
18	3,520,000	2,713,031	806,969
19	1,100,000	1,078,867	21,133
20	4,250,000	4,097,273	152,727
21	1,770,000	2,148,959	−378,959
22	3,530,000	3,617,673	−87,673
23	1,160,000	1,560,008	−400,008

However, from Exhibit 7.4 we can observe that the equation generated by the second regression produced very accurate predicted selling prices.

In other words, the majority of the transactions in our sample (17 out of 23) had asset, revenue, and cash flow value that tracked closely to each other and are, therefore, representative of where the market is.

The resulting regression equation is:

$$\text{Selling Price} = 0.029 \times \text{Rev} + 4.02 \times \text{SDE} - .90 \times \text{Inv}$$
$$+ 0.53 \text{xFF\&E} - \$684,195$$

EXHIBIT 7.4   Second Regression

Actual	Predicted	Residuals
450,000	303,305	146,695
940,000	1,174,804	−234,804
990,000	1,079,993	−89,993
530,183	531,451	−1,268
766,959	613,331	153,628
1,395,000	1,385,457	9,543
2,208,692	2,029,640	179,052
1,510,022	1,446,726	63,296
1,566,925	1,943,297	−376,372
925,000	845,852	79,148
3,500,000	3,362,447	137,553
1,150,000	1,434,909	−284,909
2,600,000	2,520,392	79,608
1,700,000	1,526,731	173,269
1,100,000	1,095,877	4,123
4,250,000	4,144,811	105,189
3,530,000	3,673,759	−143,759

Assume our subject company had the following values:

Revenue = $2,292,000	Cash Flow = $455,000
Inventory = $130,000	Fixtures & Equipment = $800,000

From the sample of transactions in Exhibit 7.2 the following values for the subject were generated by all the metrics studied thus far:

> **Multiple Variable Regression = $1,520,000**
> **Revenue Multiplier Regression = $1,238,000**
> **Cash Flow Multiplier Regression = $1,165,000**
> **Median Revenue Multiplier = $1,536,000**
> **Median Cash Flow Multiplier = $1,137,000**
> **Lower Quartile Revenue Multiplier = $1,191,000**

Lower Quartile Cash Flow Multiplier = $1,056,000
Median SDE % of the Sample = 25.9 %
Lower Quartile SDE % of Sample = 17.7 %
Subject's SDE % = 19.9 %

As we found in the chapters on revenue and cash flow multipliers, the revenue and cash flow regressions produce values that are reasonably close to each other. In this example they were only $73,200 apart ($1,238,000 – $1,165,000), whereas the medians for the two multipliers were $398,140 apart.

The two regression multipliers averaged $1,201,000 compared to the average of the two medians of $1,336,500 and the average of the two lower quartiles of $1,123,000. Is it reasonable to conclude that the $1,201,000 is the more appropriate value than $1,336,500? Given that the subject's 19.9% operating profit margin (SDE%) was well below the 25.9% median and close to lower quartile of 17.7%, it is clear that the $1,201,000 value is properly positioned.

The values in the above paragraph were just based on revenue or cash flow. The multiple variable regression brings inventory and fixtures into the calculated value. The multiple variable regression produced a value that was $319,000 higher than the average multiplier regressions. The reason for the difference can be found by comparing the subject's investment in fixtures and equipment with the sample's average investment.

The average company in the sample owned $327,916 in fixtures compared to the subject's $800,000. There were five transactions in the sample that owned more than $600,000 in fixtures. Their average revenue multiplier was 0.75 and their average cash flow multiplier was 3.02. If those two multipliers were applied to the subject, the average of the two multipliers would be $1,546,000. The multiple variable regression picked up on the fact that companies with more fixtures sold for more money. Hence, the multiple variable regression estimated value of $1,520,000 is right in line with the values suggested by the top five transactions.

The appraiser now must choose between the values calculated by the three regressions or opting to average them. If one decides that an average of the three values makes sense (I use an average 90% of the time), then the best approach is a weighted average of the three values. Since R^2 gives us an indication of which methodology was the most accurate, using the R^2 factors as the basis of weighting makes perfect sense.

The three regressions had R^2s of 0.98, 0.88, and 0.38, respectively. The total of the three factors is 2.24. Hence, the weighted average is:

Multiple Variable Regression:
$1,520,000 × 0.98/2.24 = $665,000
Revenue Multiplier Regression:
$1,238,000 × 0.88/2.24 = $486,400
Cash Flow Multiplier Regression:
$1,165,000 × 0.38/2.24 = $197,600
Total Weighted Average $1,349,000

Since the cash flow regression had the lowest R^2, it is accorded the lowest weight of the three methodologies, as it should be.

ASSET VALUES TO USE IN MULTIPLE REGRESSIONS

The values for revenue, cash flow, and inventory are readily available from three of the databases discussed in Chapter 1. Peercomps, however, does not itemize the hard assets of a transaction. Hence, inventory and fixtures and equipment[1] are combined and cannot be used in the four-variable multiple

---

[1]Note: Throughout the following discussion on fixtures, I use the word "fixtures" or "FF&E" for the combined total of furniture, fixtures, equipment, and tenant improvements.

regression methodology. If when selecting comparable trans- actions, one finds that most are from the Peercomps database, an alternative strategy is to perform a three-variable regression with hard assets (inventory and FF&E combined) being the asset variable. Just make sure that if you have transactions from other databases in your sample, you must combine the FF&E values into a single hard asset value in order to make all the transactions from different databases compatible with each other.

The FF&E values found in the remaining three databases are not as reliable as the values for inventory, revenue, and cash flow. Some of the brokers submitting transactional data will report the allocated selling price for the FF&E paid by the buyer of the business. Other brokers will report the net book value of FF&E from the balance sheet or the gross value before depre- ciation. Still others will provide an estimate of the fair market value of the FF&E. The International Business Brokers Associa- tion (IBBA) does not suggest the use of any one specific method when reporting FF&E values to the various databases.

Hence, a four-variable regression (with one variable being FF&E) can be inordinately skewed if most of the transactions in a sample were unknowingly, say, the net book value of the FF&E and the subject's value we used was gross FF&E. Consequently, the appraiser is cautioned that if the results of a four-variable regression don't look reasonable, the method should be rejected.

I have found that in samples with at least fifteen to twenty transactions all the different values reported for FF&E tend to average out. If then, the appraiser uses a "going concern value" for the subject's FF&E, the results of a regression are generally quite reasonable.

GOING CONCERN VALUE OF FF&E

The tax return depreciation schedule can be used in the fixtures and equipment analysis. However, most of a subject's fixed asset items have been fully depreciated and have a higher market value than their book value. Hence, the fixed assets should be restated to fair market value under the premise that the subject is a *going concern*, and its fixed assets are *in place, in use, and generating profits*. In other words, the fixed assets have a far greater value to the subject than if they were, say, sold piecemeal on eBay.

For example, a used computer probably would bring in less than two hundred dollars if sold on eBay. However, to the subject, that computer represents many hours of tech labor to install all the software, network to the rest of the office computers, debug, and customize. More importantly, it may have taken hundreds of hours to input all the data that is contained in its memory. That computer is technically worth thousands of dollars to the subject.

Shannon Pratt describes a common method used to value the fixtures and equipment of a going concern referred to as the "depreciated replacement cost method."[2]

The replacement cost of each asset on the company's depreciation ledger can be recalculated by adjusting its original cost by inflation to equal a current dollar value. The inflation-adjusted value for the FF&E is then prorated by its remaining life. I break down the fixed assets into the following five groups: computers, furniture and fixtures, equipment, vehicles, and tenant improvement. I then assign an average economic life to each group of assets. In the example following, the furniture and fixtures were assumed to have a fifteen-year average life, equipment a twenty-year life, vehicles a ten-year life, computers and software a seven-year life, and tenant improvements a twenty-five-year life. Given the individual circumstances of each company one appraises, it may be appropriate to increase or decrease the average useful life assigned to each classification of assets.

---

[2]Shannon P. Pratt, Robert F. Reilly, and Robert P. Schweihs, *Valuing Small Businesses and Professional Practices*, 3rd edition, New York, NY: McGraw-Hill, 1998, p. 106.

EXHIBIT 7.5 Replacement Cost Factors for Going Concern Values

			Replacement Cost Factors								
		Computers, Software 7-Year Life		Furniture & Fixtures 15-Year Life		Equipment 20-Year Life		Vehicles 10-Year Life		Tenant Improvements 25-Year Life	
Year	Cumm. Inflation	7-Year Life	Factor	15-Year Life	Factor	20-Year Life	Factor	10-Year Life	Factor	25-Year Life	Factor
2020	1.1%	92.9%	93.9%	96.7%	97.7%	97.5%	98.6%	95.0%	96.1%	98.0%	99.1%
2019	3.4%	78.6%	81.2%	90.0%	93.1%	92.5%	95.7%	85.0%	87.9%	94.0%	97.2%
2018	5.3%	64.3%	67.7%	83.3%	87.8%	87.5%	92.2%	75.0%	79.0%	90.0%	94.8%
2017	7.5%	50.0%	53.7%	76.7%	82.4%	82.5%	88.7%	65.0%	69.8%	86.0%	92.4%
2016	9.5%	35.7%	39.1%	70.0%	76.7%	77.5%	84.9%	55.0%	60.2%	82.0%	89.8%
2015	10.2%	21.4%	23.6%	63.3%	69.8%	72.5%	79.9%	45.0%	49.6%	78.0%	85.9%
2014	10.8%	7.1%	7.9%	56.7%	62.8%	67.5%	74.8%	35.0%	38.8%	74.0%	82.0%
2013	12.3%	0.0%	0.0%	50.0%	56.2%	62.5%	70.2%	25.0%	28.1%	70.0%	78.6%
2012	14.1%	0.0%	0.0%	43.3%	49.4%	57.5%	65.6%	15.0%	17.1%	66.0%	75.3%
2011	17.2%	0.0%	0.0%	36.7%	43.0%	52.5%	61.5%	10.0%	11.7%	62.0%	72.6%
2010	18.6%	0.0%	0.0%	30.0%	35.6%	47.5%	56.3%	10.0%	11.9%	58.0%	68.8%
2009	21.4%	0.0%	0.0%	23.3%	28.3%	42.5%	51.6%	10.0%	12.1%	54.0%	65.6%
2008	21.4%	0.0%	0.0%	16.7%	20.2%	37.5%	45.5%	10.0%	12.1%	50.0%	60.7%
2007	25.5%	0.0%	0.0%	10.0%	12.6%	32.5%	40.8%	10.0%	12.6%	46.0%	57.7%
2006	28.0%	0.0%	0.0%	0.0%	0.0%	27.5%	35.2%	10.0%	12.8%	42.0%	53.8%
2005	31.4%	0.0%	0.0%	0.0%	0.0%	22.5%	29.6%	10.0%	13.1%	38.0%	49.9%
2004	34.7%	0.0%	0.0%	0.0%	0.0%	17.5%	23.6%	10.0%	13.5%	34.0%	45.8%
2003	36.7%	0.0%	0.0%	0.0%	0.0%	12.5%	17.1%	10.0%	13.7%	30.0%	41.0%
2002	39.2%	0.0%	0.0%	0.0%	0.0%	10.0%	13.9%	10.0%	13.9%	26.0%	36.2%

EXHIBIT 7.6 Going Concern Values of a Company's FF&E

Year	Total Fixed Assets & Tenant Improvements		Computers, Software 7-Year Life		Furniture & Fixtures 15-Year Life		Equipment 20-Year Life		Vehicles 10-Year Life		Tenant Improvements 25-Year Life	
	Ledger Totals	Adjusted Totals	Ledger Totals	Adjusted Totals	Ledger Totals	Adjusted Totals	Ledger Totals	Adjusted Totals	Ledger Totals	Adjusted Totals	Ledger Totals	Adjusted Totals
Totals	267,716	99,224	0	0	3,227	0	4,279	3,440	260,210	95,784	22,500	14,760
2020	0	0		0		0		0		0		0
2019	0	0		0		0		0	0	0		0
2018	30,290	23,929		0		0		0	30,290	23,929		0
2017	31,087	22,104		0		0	2,146	1,904	28,941	20,201		0
2016	4,058	2,443		0		0		0	4,058	2,443		0
2015	30,015	14,887		0		0		0	30,015	14,887		0
2014	35,600	14,123		0		0	861	644	34,739	13,479		0
2013	27,034	8,132		0		0	1,272	893	25,762	7,239		0
2012	0	0		0		0		0		0		0
2011	0	0		0		0		0		0		0
2010	44,226	5,263		0		0		0	44,226	5,263		0
2009	0	0		0		0		0		0	22,500	14,760
2008	0	0		0		0		0		0		0
2007	0	0		0		0		0		0		0
2006	24,977	3,197		0		0		0	24,977	3,197		0
2005	4,072	419		0	872	0		0	3,200	419		0
2004	0	0		0		0		0		0		0
2003	0	0		0		0		0		0		0
2002	36,357	4,726		0	2,355	0		0	34,002	4,726		0

Exhibit 7.5 shows the replacement cost adjustment factors used to prorate the remaining value of an asset adjusted by inflation. For example, a $100 desk purchased in 2015 (shaded in gray) would have an expected life of fifteen years. The equivalent replacement cost today adjusted for inflation would be $110.20 ($100 × (1 + 10.2%)). However, its prorated remaining life (using mid-year convention) is 63.3% [(15 years–5.5 years)/15 years]. Therefore, the replacement cost value adjusted for inflation is $69.75 ($110.20 × 63.3%).

The actual cost of the assets on the subject company's fixtures and equipment ledger adjusted by the above factors yields the replacement cost value as follows:

The gross cost of the subject company's FF&E in the previous exhibit was $267,716. The going concern value for all the assets was $99,224.

When using multiple variable regression with FF&E as one of the independent variables, the going concern value for a company's FF&E tends to sync up with average calculation of FF&E for all the transactions in a sample. Again, the appraiser is cautioned to use his or her good judgment when employing the multiple variable regression methodology. If the results do not appear reasonable, the methodology should be rejected.

The reader may request the Excel template that creates the two previous tables by emailing the author at fred@fredhall.biz.

CHAPTER 8

Selection of Transactions in the Sample

The old axiom "garbage in, garbage out" is especially true when selecting transactions for samples to be used in regression analysis. It only takes one or two outlier transactions in a sample to skew the results inappropriately. This can be the case when using medians or averages of a sample but even more so with regression. In appraisal school, our instructors suggested we build a sample by selecting every comparable transaction within the subject company's SIC (Standard Industrial Classification) code. The explanation was that in doing so, opposing experts could not challenge us for having cherry-picked transactions for our sample. Cherry-picking was a challenge occasionally used by attorneys to discredit an appraiser's results.

This is false logic because the result would be a sample with companies generating $500,000 in revenue alongside companies earning $5,000,000 in revenue. Business appraisers need to take a page from the real estate appraisers' playbook. A real estate appraiser would never consider comparing a 5,000 sq. ft. house to a 1,000 sq. ft. house. The two houses have completely different construction costs, quality of materials, and are in totally different markets. A 5,000 sq. ft. house is likely to be in a very wealthy neighborhood; not so much for a 1,000 sq. ft. house. Likewise, in business appraisals there is no way a $5,000,000 transaction has any similarity to a $500,000 transaction. Their balance sheets and P&Ls are completely different and all their ratios are completely different. Yet, I frequently find samples collected by appraisers with revenues farther apart than that.

REVENUE RANGE

Using a company's operating profit margin (SDE%) as a predictor of its multipliers involves several considerations. First, the revenue range of the transactions that are selected should be fairly narrow, and the average revenue for the sample should be fairly close in size to that of the subject.

From the analysis in Exhibit 8.1,[1] we can see that the cash flow and revenue multipliers tend to increase with the size of the company. Therefore, using a sample of $5 million companies to compare to a $500,000 company would more than likely overvalue the subject. The balance sheets, income statements, and all the operating ratios for $5 million companies are significantly

EXHIBIT 8.1 Size Effect on Multipliers and SDE%

Total Transactions	Total Sales Range		Median CF Mult.	Median Rev Mult.	Median SDE% (%)
9,883	$0	$500,000	1.96	0.50	25.9
4,280	$500,000	$1,000,000	2.35	0.43	19.1
2,754	$1,000,001	$2,000,000	2.64	0.41	16.3
1,588	$2,000,001	$5,000,000	2.97	0.42	14.3
384	$5,000,001	$8,000,000	3.53	0.44	12.7
506	$8,000,000	$25,000,000	4.44	0.53	12.7
315	$25,000,001	$99,000,000	5.55	0.68	12.5
	All Transactions				
19,710		$603,463	2.32	0.47	20.7

[1]Data was taken from the DealStat's database. The database was filtered by removing all stock sales, transactions with operating losses, or cash flow multipliers greater than 10.

different from $500,000 companies. As such, companies that are either significantly larger than or significantly smaller than the subject are not relevant comparables.

We also see from Exhibit 8.1 that the operating profit margins (SDE%) decrease as the size of the companies increase. This occurs because in smaller companies, the owner typically manages all facets of the company. He or she is the salesperson, marketing manager, HR manager, and bookkeeper. All the profits flow to the owner as compensation for all these jobs. As we see from Exhibit 8.1, a $500,000 company would generate cash flow at an average of 25.9% for every dollar of revenue, or $129,500. Also, $500,000 companies sell for an average of 1.96 times their earnings, which would suggest a selling price of $253,820.

For this company to grow to $5 million, however, the owner must now hire a bookkeeper, an HR manager, and possibly a CFO. The company is now too big for the owner to do everything. A $5 million company typically earns $715,000 in discretionary earnings ($5 million × 14.3% [from Exhibit 7.1]). Thus, when a company grows from $500,000 to $5 million, the additional $4.5 million in sales added $585,500 in earnings, which only yields an SDE% of 13% ($585,500 ÷ $4,500,000).

Thus, the $5 million company in the example produced higher levels of gross revenues and discretionary earnings yet earned a lower SDE%. The importance of this peculiarity is that in using SDE% to predict the multipliers of a business, it becomes increasingly important to select a sample of comparables that are as close in revenue size to the subject as possible and that are from similar SIC classifications. Otherwise, we might look at the 25.9% SDE% of a $500,000 company and draw the false conclusion that it deserves better market value multipliers than the $5 million, which only produced an SDE% of 14.3%.

When selecting a sample, start by filtering the list of transactions for a revenue range of one-third less than the subject to 50% more than the subject.

Hence, for a $2 million subject company we would begin searching for transactions ranging from $1,400,000 to $3,000,000. If the initial search produced a sample of, say, 50 transactions, I recommend reducing the search criteria to $1,500,000 to $2,500,000.

A small homogeneous sample of 15 to 25 observations will generally be much more statistically relevant than a large diverse sample.

WHAT HAPPENS WHEN THE SAMPLE IS TOO SMALL?

After one filters a sample for all the issues discussed in this chapter, it is conceivable that the sample would have less than the minimum of 12 to 15 transactions that we would prefer to have. I have used all the regression methodologies discussed in this book for samples as small as eight. But the risk of misreading the market becomes much greater, as it does when using medians or quartiles with small samples. So the question is, how do we handle samples that appear to be too small?

After applying all the filters discussed in this chapter, if one can only find ten or twelve comparables, try increasing your range of SIC codes first. If you initially selected SIC 1799 (Specialty Trade Contractors), try increasing the range from 1751 (Carpentry Work) to 1799. Try to run the two regressions on this sample. If the first regression produces a good R^2 without removing any outliers, consider using that regression. If you only need to remove one or two outliers for the second regression and it produces a much higher R^2, then use the second regression.

After testing the above samples, then, build a new sample with just SIC 1799, but increase the range of revenue you initially selected. For a $2 million company your initial selection range might be $1.5 million to $2.5 million. Try a range of $1 million to $3 million. Run the two regressions on this sample and compare it to the results you obtained on the wider SIC range. Select which sample produced the best R^2. When all else fails you may have to combine the two expanded samples—a wider SIC and wider revenue.

If you increased the sample by increasing the SIC range, be prepared to defend your choice. Anyone reviewing your list of transactions will raise the challenge that there are many transactions that are not similar to the subject. Here is my response to such challenges. It works every time, so commit it to memory:

The unique characteristics of the subject company are why a customer came to it, it is not necessarily why a buyer came to the company. The Guideline Company Transaction Method is a buyer-driven methodology. It is the buyer who places the offer on the table. A buyer's search criteria are very wide. Hence, we can also employ a wide search criterion for our sample in the same manner that the buyer does.

It is very common that a buyer may start out looking for, say, a hardware store to buy. When none are available that fit his requirements, he then begins searching for nurseries, auto part stores, and industrial supply businesses. None of these are really similar companies, but the buyer's primary concern when searching for a business is to find one he can afford that will provide the lifestyle to which he is accustomed. As you can see, he is applying the same criteria to all those different businesses.

My favorite story of a buyer's search criteria occurred when I was a business broker in Sacramento. A buyer inquired about a grocery store I had listed in Oregon, some 600 miles north. An offer was made and accepted, but two weeks before the close of escrow the seller died. The store went into probate and the buyer, not wishing to wait a year, backed out of the deal. He came back to my office and asked, "What else do you have?" He ended up buying an X-ray technician company 500 miles east in the state of Nevada. How does a buyer go from a grocery store to an X-ray technician company and from California to Oregon and finally to Nevada? In my many years as a business broker, this phenomenon was not uncommon. The only similarity between these two businesses was that both produced the same level of income for the given selling price—basically, the same logic the market approach methodology applies.

CASH FLOW MULTIPLIER RANGE

If the subject is reasonably profitable, the selected sample should not contain companies with negative cash flow or very low-level cash flow (generally companies with cash flow multipliers greater than 10.0). Companies that do not produce sufficient cash flow to pay the debt service on a loan or the owner's salary are generally not sold on the basis of cash flow but rather, the value of their hard assets. Hence, their cash flow and revenue multipliers are not relevant comparisons to the subject that is profitable.

In support of restricting the sample to transactions that are profitable and have cash flow multipliers less than 10.0, one should mention in his or her appraisal that the premise of value for the appraisal is a "going concern." Transactions with little or no cash flow that cannot afford to pay an owner a salary are in danger of failure and therefore, do not meet the criteria of a "going concern."

Conversely, if your subject is not profitable, you should consider selecting comparables with operating losses or very low-level cash flow (cash flow multipliers greater than 10.0).

This selection process in not cherry-picking. It is selecting transactions that are relevant comparisons to the subject. The regression methodologies attempt to determine the appropriate multipliers for companies given the level of profits of the subject. A sample cluttered with transactions that lost money will not produce reasonable multipliers for a profitable subject.

Thus, I recommend excluding all transactions with negative cash flow profit margins or low-profit companies with a cash flow multiplier greater than 10.0.

INVENTORY LEVELS

If the subject company carries inventory that is an integral part of its operations, the transactions one selects should also show inventory. These are typically companies that are retail, wholesale, or manufacturing businesses.

A great many transactions in these three SIC groups in the DealStats, Bizcomps, and ValuSource databases report that there was no inventory transferred in the sale. It seems unlikely that companies such as retailers or wholesalers would not have any inventory. However, when analyzing SIC codes 5000 to 5999 (wholesale and retail companies), 21% of the 6,273 companies in Bizcomps' database were listed as having been sold with no inventory. Of the 8,800 companies in DealStats database that were in SIC codes 5000 to 5999, 30% claim to have been sold with no inventory.

Having been a business broker for 16 years in an office with 15 other brokers, I have found that in many listings the commissions were calculated on all assets being sold excluding inventory. The selling broker instructed the buyers and sellers to handle the transfer of inventory outside of escrow between themselves. The buyer and seller had to count the inventory and handle any financing documentation without the selling broker's assistance. As a result, the purchase agreements indicated that the selling price did not include inventory and the escrow documents showed that no inventory was sold in the transaction. In addition, there was also no documentation for any seller carryback. The selling broker then submits the transaction to a database and reports that the subject generated $1,000,000 in revenue and sold for $400,000, hence, a 0.40 revenue multiplier. The broker who represented the buyer in the sale submits the same transaction to the various databases and notes that the selling price was $400,000 plus $200,000 in inventory, hence, a revenue multiplier of 0.60.

Bizcomps posts all of the transactions to its database with selling prices that exclude inventory. Hence, regardless of the amount of inventory that the transaction reports indicate, the cash flow and revenue multipliers from Bizcomps data are always calculated with no inventory included in the selling price.

However, 79% of the transactions listed in Bizcomps also report the amount of inventory that was transferred in the sale. Consequently, we can calculate the asset sale price by adding inventory to Bizcomps' selling price. The transaction can then be included in the same sample with DealStats or ValuSource deals at which time the transactions with zero reported inventory become a problem.

DealStats and ValuSource present their data differently. For example, a business broker submitting transactional data to DealStats might indicate that the selling price was $600,000, which included $200,000 in inventory, and the company's revenue and SDE were $1,000,000 and $200,000 respectively. DealStats would post the MVIC (Market Value of Invested Capital is DealStats' name for the selling price) as $600,000, the corresponding revenue multiplier would be 0.60 ($600,000 / $1,000,000), and the cash flow multiplier would be 3.0 ($600,000 / $200,000). However, if the broker allowed the seller and buyer to handle inventory outside of escrow, he might report the same transaction as having a selling price of $400,000 with no inventory being transferred. DealStats would post MVIC as $400,000 in this case, the resulting revenue multiplier would be 0.40 ($400,000 / $1,000,000), and the cash flow multiplier would be 2.0 ($400,000 / $200,000).

It is common practice for appraisers to only show the revenue, cash flow, and selling prices of transactions in their appraisals and ignore inventory and fixtures and equipment values. Hence, the appraiser and anyone reading the report will assume that the selling prices for all comparables obtained from DealStats or ValuSource included inventory that was transferred in the sale.

If the appraiser only used the Bizcomps database for his sample of comparables, all the Bizcomps selling prices are reported excluding inventory. Consequently, the multipliers and the resulting values calculated from those transactions will also assume no inventory was transferred. Hence, if one used the 0.40 multiplier from the first example to value a subject with $1,500,000 in revenue and $200,000 in inventory, the resulting value would be $1,500,000 × 0.40 = $600,000. However, the appraiser would then have to add the subject's $200,000 in inventory to arrive at the total asset sale price of $800,000.

However, if one had combined Bizcomps and DealStats transactions into a single sample, then transactions with no inventory reported become a major problem. To make the selling price in the Bizcomps transactions compatible with DealStats, one must add inventory to the Bizcomps selling prices. As we noted above, 21% of Bizcomps' transactions showed zero inventory.

From Exhibit 8.2 we can clearly see that transactions that reported inventory being transferred had cash flow and revenue multipliers that were 15% to 18% higher than those transactions that reported no inventory. Cash flow multipliers for DealStats transactions with inventory reported an average of 2.31 compared to 1.98 without inventory. Bizcomps transactions with inventory averaged a 2.09 cash flow multiplier, whereas those transactions with no inventory reported a 1.77 cash flow multiplier.

It seems like it should be obvious that the multipliers would be higher when including inventory in the selling price. The fact

EXHIBIT 8.2 Multipliers with Inventory vs. without Inventory

	DealStats			Bizcomps		
	Sample Size	Median Cash Flow Mult.	Median Revenue Mult.	Sample Size	Median Cash Flow Mult.	Median Revenue Mult.
Inv = 0	2,086	1.98	0.32	1,166	1.77	0.34
Inv > 0	5,697	2.31	0.37	4,601	2.09	0.40

is, appraisers never show inventory or fixtures values in their appraisal data when they build a sample of transactions. All we are shown is revenue, cash flow, and the selling price. We are to assume that the selling prices of all the transactions include inventory. However, with such a high percentage of transactions that are reported with no mention of inventory, one can surely bet that most samples in valuations have a mix of both transactions.

Therefore, when building your sample, either select all transactions with no inventory in the selling price or select all transactions that reported that inventory was included in the selling price. Do not mix the two types of transactions in the same sample.

As a side bar, if you opt to select transactions with no inventory reported in the selling price, the resulting value for your subject will be sans inventory. You must then add inventory to your subject's value to obtain the total value of the business.

There are many types of businesses where inventory is an insignificant asset. Restaurants, for example, carry inventory. However, it is usually only a few thousand dollars, and it is quite conceivable that the business really did sell with no inventory. In situations like this, mixing transactions with and without inventory is acceptable. The appraiser should use his or her good judgment when selecting transactions that normally carry large amounts of inventory.

FIXTURES AND EQUIPMENT

Fixtures and equipment is another datapoint reported by most of the databases that is also generally overlooked. It is not as critical to the valuation process as inventory. However, it does provide us with another point of analysis to fine-tune our sample. Exhibit 8.3 following illustrates a very common occurrence. Transaction #15 shaded in gray is a classic example. Is there anything about this company's revenue or cash flow that would explain the $1,200,000 selling price?

EXHIBIT 8.3 Fixtures and Equipment Outliers

	Selling Price (b)	Gross Rev. (c)	CF (SDE) (d)	SDE% (d) ÷ (c)	Rev. Mult. (b) ÷ (c)	CF Mult. (b) ÷ (d)	Invent. (e)	Fixtures (f)
1	175,000	1,050,000	30,000	2.9%	0.17	5.83	55,000	125,000
2	200,000	950,000	45,000	4.7%	0.21	4.44	53,000	300,000
3	225,000	875,000	50,000	5.7%	0.26	4.50	12,000	688,000
4	201,000	877,000	55,000	6.3%	0.23	3.65	142,000	102,000
5	205,000	774,000	50,000	6.5%	0.26	4.10	25,000	47,000
6	300,000	979,000	67,000	6.8%	0.31	4.48	30,000	36,000
7	415,000	1,490,000	110,000	7.4%	0.28	3.77	35,000	144,000
8	650,000	1,279,000	125,000	9.8%	0.51	5.20	15,000	516,000
9	425,000	1,113,000	110,000	9.9%	0.38	3.86	43,000	419,000
10	350,000	876,000	100,000	11.4%	0.40	3.50	12,000	500,000
11	205,000	774,000	95,000	12.3%	0.26	2.16	38,000	67,000
12	775,000	975,000	175,000	17.9%	0.79	4.43	25,000	25,000
13	485,000	1,205,000	255,000	21.2%	0.40	1.90	100,000	5,000
14	220,000	550,000	125,000	22.7%	0.40	1.76	20,000	250,000
15	1,200,000	1,000,000	250,000	25.0%	1.20	4.80	50,000	1,000,000
16	285,000	572,000	157,000	27.4%	0.50	1.82	25,000	150,000
17	275,000	505,000	169,000	33.5%	0.54	1.63	90,000	250,000
18	725,000	1,156,000	391,000	33.8%	0.63	1.85	82,000	168,000
19	565,000	959,000	325,000	33.9%	0.59	1.74	20,000	353,000
20	475,000	714,000	245,000	34.3%	0.67	1.94	30,000	255,000
21	950,000	1,222,000	425,000	34.8%	0.78	2.24	157,000	256,000
22	925,000	1,021,000	360,000	35.3%	0.91	2.57	30,000	354,000
23	1,050,000	1,220,000	575,000	47.1%	0.86	1.83	20,000	150,000
	2 standard deviations =			46.0%			128,335	742,545
	Median				0.40	3.50		
	Multipliers without comp #15			Median	0.40	3.03		

Clearly the buyer was willing to pay a premium for this business because it was carrying $1,000,000 in fixtures and equipment. As a result, the revenue and cash flow multipliers were extraordinarily high, but revenue and cash flow had nothing to do with it. All the methodologies used in the Market Approach are oriented toward determining an appropriate multiple for the subject's revenue and cash flow. The multipliers transaction #15 earned had nothing to do with revenue or cash flow.

The median cash flow multiplier for the whole sample in Exhibit 8.3 including #15 was 3.50. If we removed that one transaction, the median multiplier drops to 3.03. Had we left #15 in the sample, we may have overvalued our subject by more than 10%. Regression analysis would have removed that transaction as an outlier. However, if you were not using regression analysis, an attempt to remove that transaction from the sample might be labeled "cherry-picking."

How does one avoid the semblance of cherry-picking when using conventional methodologies? Consider calculating two standard deviations for data in the columns of inventory, FF&E, and SDE%. Two standard deviations represent the highest 2.5% of values in the column of data. The SDE% column produced a 2x standard deviation of 46%. Is it possible that a company could generate that level of profitability? Certainly. Is it reasonable? Hardly. The most profitable transaction in the above sample was #23, which earned a 47.1% profit margin. Theoretically, less than 2.5% of all transactions in that SIC code could achieve that level of cash flow. In fact, the next six most profitable companies in the sample all earned an SDE% in a low to middle 30% range, considerably less than transaction #23's 47.1% profit margin. This transaction appears too good to be true, and it undoubtedly is. It should be removed from the sample as an outlier, and two times the standard deviation is a good break point. It is quite common for brokers to miscalculate a company's cash flow or report gross profits rather than SDE when submitting a transaction to the databases. It is also common that they exaggerated SDE to make their listings more attractive. Again, this is a transaction that a regression would automatically identify as an outlier.

The fixtures column produced a 2x standard deviation of $742,545. There was just one transaction that exceeded that level: #15. There were just two transactions in the inventory column that exceeded the two standard deviation break point. It is a good practice to remove the transactions that exceed two standard deviations *before* you do the regressions. Don't delegate all the heavy lifting to the regression. You will get much better results by doing minor housekeeping of your sample before running an analysis. Had you left those four obvious outliers in the sample, your first regression would have produced an R^2 of 0.55 and the second regression an R^2 of 0.82. With those outliers already removed, the first regression would have produced an R^2 of 0.64 and the second a 0.91.

STOCK SALES VS. ASSET SALES

Bizcomps, ValuSource, and Peercomps[2] all report that the selling prices for transactions listed in their respective databases are asset sale values or have been converted to asset sale values.[3,4] An asset sale value is generally considered to be the value of a company's three main assets: fixtures and equipment (FF&E), inventory, and all intangibles. DealStats procedural manual defines MVIC as: "the total consideration paid to the seller and includes any cash, notes and/or securities that were used as a form of payment plus any interest-bearing liabilities assumed by the buyer." The MVIC price includes the noncompete value and the assumption of any interest-bearing liabilities. MVIC excludes: (1) the real estate value; (2) any earnouts (because they have not yet been earned, and they may not be earned); and (3) the employment/consulting agreement values.[5] Thus, it is possible that the mix of assets or liabilities comprised in MVIC might be significantly different than the three assets in an asset sale value.

---

[2]Bizcomps and DealStats® data are obtained from the Business Valuation Resources website: www.bvmarketdata.com; ValuSource data is obtained from the ValuSource website: www.valusource.com; and Peercomps data is obtained from the Peercomps® website: www.peercomps.com.
[3]Jack Sanders, "Bizcomps User Guide," 2004, pp. 6 and 12. Bizcomps does not include inventory in its sale price. However, it is a simple matter to add the value of inventory to obtain an equivalent asset sale price.
[4]Peercomps, "How it Works\Data Gathering Process\Transactional Data," https://www.peercomps.com/.
[5]DealStats FAQs: "What is the legend for DealStats transaction and other data?" www.bvresources.com/products/faqs/dealstats Pg. 5.

The majority of smaller companies with revenues less than, say, $4 million are sold as asset sales. However, in many of the smaller transactions listed by DealStats, the submitting brokers did not identify the value of the assets being transferred. As a result, we are left with the assumption that MVIC equals an asset sale value, which might not always be the case. For larger companies with revenues in excess of, say, $4 million, various combinations of assets and liabilities are often acquired by the buyer. Hence, MVIC for these larger transactions is frequently different than an asset sale value. However, the transactional data for many of those sales may enable the appraiser to reconcile MVIC to an equivalent asset sale value.

MVIC often takes on many dissimilar forms that can be significantly different from asset sale values. In fact, there are at least five different variations of selling prices that are identified as MVIC in the DealStats database. An asset sale price is by far the most common. However, four other possible MVIC variations (transactions "b" to "e" in Exhibit 8.4) are radically different from each other. Those transactions should not be included in the same sample with other transactions where an asset sale value is the desired conclusion of value. If left in a sample, the resulting valuation may be significantly skewed.

The exhibit below shows a typical balance sheet of a company and the combination of assets and liabilities that might have been acquired by a buyer. Depending on the combination of assets and liabilities acquired in the sale, the submitting broker might have reported a selling price ranging from $2,200,000 to $3,700,000. Bizcomps and ValuSource attempt to reconstruct the broker's selling data to reflect an asset sale price; DealStats does not. All five of the variations in Exhibit 8.4 would be identified as MVIC in the DealStats database. As we can see, the resulting cash flow multipliers (selling price ÷ cash flow) for each transaction are significantly different as are the revenue multipliers (selling price ÷ revenue).

If we assume that the company in Exhibit 8.4 generated $800,000 in cash flow, the cash flow multiplier for an asset sale

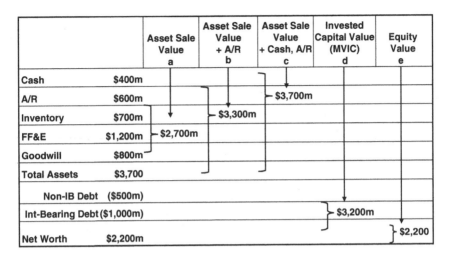

		Asset Sale Value a	Asset Sale Value + A/R b	Asset Sale Value + Cash, A/R c	Invested Capital Value (MVIC) d	Equity Value e
Cash	$400m					
A/R	$600m			$3,700m		
Inventory	$700m		$3,300m			
FF&E	$1,200m	$2,700m				
Goodwill	$800m					
Total Assets	$3,700					
Non-IB Debt	($500m)					
Int-Bearing Debt	($1,000m)				$3,200m	
Net Worth	$2,200m					$2,200

EXHIBIT 8.4 Different MVIC Values

(transaction "a") would be 3.38 ($2,700,000 ÷ $800,000), and the revenue multiplier would be 0.675 ($2,700,000 ÷ $4,000,000). If the buyer acquired all the assets of the company (as in transaction "c"), the submitting broker might report the selling price as $3,700,000. Hence, the resulting cash flow multiplier would be 4.625, and the revenue multiplier would be 0.925. The multipliers from transaction "c" are over 36% higher than the multipliers for an asset sale. Consequently, if an appraiser collected a sample of nine transactions that reported asset sale values (as in transaction "a") and then added transaction "c" to the sample, the resulting average multiplier of the sample would be increased, thus overstating the value of the subject.

In the last two years DealStats has made great strides in reporting the value of the assets and liabilities that were transferred in a transaction. Over 55% of the 30,000 transactions listed in DealStats' database now have a Purchase Price Allocation Data section listing all the assets and liabilities that were transferred to the buyer. Unfortunately, only 31.8% of the transactions identified as stock sales included a breakout for the Purchase Price Allocation. Additional information regarding the asset values of the transaction is available in the Notes section. It is, therefore, critical that the appraiser read the Purchase Price Allocation section and the Notes section appended to each transaction report to obtain a full understanding of the structure of the sale.

All of the comparables selected for one's sample should be homogenous. If all the transactions in one's sample list asset sale selling prices (as in transaction "a"), then transaction "c" must be reconciled to reflect an asset sale selling price before it can be included in the sample. Hence, in transaction "c" above, one would deduct the value of cash and A/R from MVIC to arrive at an equivalent asset sale value ($3,700,000 – $600,000 – $400,000 = $2,700,000).

To illustrate the importance of reading the DealStats notes and reconciling transactions to asset sale selling prices, I downloaded all the transactions in SIC codes 3000 to 3999 from all three databases. The objective was to determine the percentage of companies in which Dealstats' MVIC did not equal an asset sale selling price. The selling prices from the Bizcomps and ValuSource databases were reconciled to include FF&E, inventory, and goodwill and exclude earn-outs and employment contracts. (Note: I added the value of inventory to Bizcomp's selling prices to be comparable to ValuSource and DealStats' asset sale prices.) Hopefully, DealStats' MVIC will match the selling prices of ValuSource and Bizcomps transactions.

Of the 2,474 transactions found with those SIC codes, 1,120 were from the DealStats database, 381 from Bizcomps, 291 from Peercomps, and 682 from ValuSource. Of the 1,120 DealStats transactions 10% (111) had duplications in Bizcomps or ValuSource. Since ValuSource and Bizcomps only report asset sale selling prices, if DealStats' MVIC matches ValuSource's or Bizcomps' selling price, we can assume that MVIC is also an asset sale price. Upon inspection of the 111 duplications, I found that 37% of the DealStats MVIC values did not match the corresponding asset sale price of the ValuSource or Bizcomps transaction. Fortunately, from the Purchase Price Allocation data section included in the DealStats transaction reports, I was able to reconcile the MVIC value to an equivalent asset sale price in all but 13% of the transactions.

Of critical importance are transactions that are listed as stock sales. Of the 1,120 DealStats transactions analyzed, 111 were duplications, but only 8 of those duplications were stock sales. There were an additional 455 DealStats transactions in those SIC codes that were listed as stock sales of which 212 had no purchase price allocation. The remaining 243 contained a breakout for the Purchase Price Allocation that enabled us to reconcile the transactions to an equivalent asset sale selling price. After reconciling the Purchase Price Allocation of the 243 stock sale transactions, I found that 78% had MVIC values that were different from a reconciled asset sale price. We can probably assume that the stock sale transactions that had no allocation data will have a similar percentage of MVIC values that do not match the equivalent asset sale value. Thus, between the stock sales and duplications we found where MVIC did not match an asset sale price, we might expect that as much as 35% of the DealStats database has MVIC values that are different from asset sale values.

Consequently, it is imperative that an appraiser reads the notes and allocation data in the DealStats transaction reports to reconcile MVIC to an equivalent asset sale price, if an asset sale price is the desired conclusion of value. Failing to do so means that possibly 1/3 of your sample may contain inflated MVIC values that will skew your resulting multipliers. Even if one made all the possible adjustments for asset sale prices, a typical sample of 20 to 30 transactions will undoubtedly still have a half dozen or more MVIC values where no allocation data was available. Odds are that several of them had MVIC values that were not equal to asset sale values. Using the median to determine the sample's multipliers may eliminate the effect of these outliers. But the better solution is to eliminate all DealStats transactions that can't be reconciled to asset sale values.

Regardless, the appraiser is cautioned that when the MVIC value for a transaction can't be reconciled and looks too good to be true, it probably is and, therefore, should be rejected. In addition, since the high percentage of stock sale transactions have MVIC values that were not asset sale values, all stock sale transactions should be rejected when the appropriate Purchase Price Allocation Data section is not available.

Exhibits 8.5 and 8.6 are portions of typical transaction reports from DealStats and how to reconcile the data to asset sale values.

EXHIBIT 8.5   Typical Transaction Report Data from DealStats

DealStats		Source Data	
Transaction Detail		Broker Name:	Emmett, Donald
		Broker Firms Name	Entrust Associates
Years in Business	16		
Number of Employees	15		
NAICS Codes		Contact Broker (Retrieve broker	
332312 - Fabricated Structural		contact information from BVR's	
Metal		"Find a Broker" database)	
Asking Price	$2,750,000	Amount of Down Payment:	$1,625,000
MVIC	$2,000,000	Stock or Asset Sale:	Asset
Debt Assumed	$0	Transaction Costs:	N/A
Balance Sheet Data		Purchase Price Allocation Data	
Balance Sheet Date	12/31/14	PPA Date	08/30/15
Cash Equivalents	$878,784	Cash Equivalents	$0
Trade Receivables	$250,904	Trade Receivables	$210,000
Inventory	$19,743	Inventory	$85,000
Other Current Assets	$30,321	Other Current Assets	$0
Total Current Assets	$1,179,785	Total Current Assets	$295,000
Fixed Assets	$40,259	Fixed Assets	$550,000
Real Estate	n/a	Real Estate	$0
Intangibles	n/a	Identifiable Intangibles	
Other Noncurrent Assets	n/a	Non-compete	$50,000
Total Assets	$1,220,011	Goodwill	$1,105,000
Current Liabilities	$52,695	Total Intangibles	$1,155,000
Long-Term Liabilities	$16,937	Other Noncurrent Assets	
Total Liabilities	$69,632	Total Assets	$2,000,000
Stockholders' Equity	$1,150,379	Interest-bearing Liabilities	
		Total Liabilities	

Source: Data from DealStats.

EXHIBIT 8.6 Typical Stock Sale Data from DealStats

DealStats		Source Data	
Transaction Detail		Broker Name:	Woolley, Charles
		Broker Firms Name	Kingsley Group Business Svc
Years in Business	9		
Number of Employees	12		
NAICS Codes		Contact Broker (Retrieve broker contact	
332312 - Fabricated Structural		information from BVR's "Find a Broker"	
Metal		database)	
Asking Price	n/a	Amount of Down Payment:	$236,777
MVIC	$736,777	Stock or Asset Sale:	Stock
Debt Assumed	$0	Transaction Costs:	n/a
Balance Sheet Data		Purchase Price Allocation Data	
Balance Sheet Date	12/31/14	PPA Date	n/a
Cash Equivalents	$878,784	Cash Equivalents	n/a
Trade Receivables	$250,904	Trade Receivables	n/a
Inventory	$19,743	Inventory	n/a
Other Current Assets	$30,321	Other Current Assets	n/a
Total Current Assets	$1,179,785	Total Current Assets	n/a
Fixed Assets	$40,259	Fixed Assets	n/a
Real Estate	n/a	Real Estate	n/a
Intangibles	n/a	Identifiable Intangibles	n/a
Other Noncurrent Assets	n/a	Non-compete	n/a
Total Assets	$1,220,011	Goodwill	n/a
Current Liabilities	$52,695	Total Intangibles	n/a
Long-Term Liabilities	$16,937	Other Noncurrent Assets	n/a
Total Liabilities	$69,632	Total Assets	n/a
Stockholders' Equity	$1,150,379	Interest-bearing Liabilities	n/a
		Total Liabilities	n/a

Source: Data from DealStats.

In Exhibit 8.5, MVIC ("Market Value of Invested Capital" is DealStats' selling price) is reported as $2,000,000; however, that price included $210,000 in receivables. MVIC must be reconciled to an asset sale value, which is $1,790,000 ($85,000 + $550,000 + $1,155,000).

In Exhibit 8.6 there is no purchase price allocation. Since the transaction is listed as a stock sale, it is highly likely that other assets or liabilities were transferred in the sale in addition to the three standard asset sale assets. All stock sale transactions should be rejected when there is no indication of what was transferred in the sale.

TRANSACTIONS WITH REAL ESTATE

Most of the databases will report if real estate was sold with the business. All the databases claim they do not include real estate value with the value of the business. However, I have found many transactions where the real estate value was accidentally combined with the business value. Hence, when a transaction report notes that real estate was also sold to the buyer, if the selling price of the business looks too good to be true, it probably included the real estate value.

Regardless, transactions with real estate are possibly not relevant transactions for our sample. After buyer and seller initially negotiate a price for the business and the real estate, the buyer will then go to his banker for a loan. Banks will often quote a higher interest rate and shorter term on the business part of the transaction than on the real estate part. Once the buyer becomes aware of this, he will ask the seller to renegotiate the price. If the original terms were $1,000,000 for the real estate and $800,000 for the business, the buyer might request that the real estate be increased to $1,200,000 and the business decreased to $600,000. The shift saves the buyer a significant amount of debt service and costs the seller nothing. Hence, the seller agrees.

Exhibit 8.7 suggests that revenue multipliers for transactions that included real estate were lower than transactions without real estate. The inference here is that selling prices of the businesses that involved real estate were manipulated downward by the buyer and seller. The sample size of 813 for

EXHIBIT 8.7 Transactions with Real Estate

	DealStats	
Transaction Type	Sample Size	Median Revenue Multiplier
Sold with Real Estate	813	0.42
Sold without Real Estate	19,000	0.47

transactions sold with real estate is quite small compared to the sample size of 19,000 for transactions sold without real estate, which might explain the difference. Hence, we can't make a definitive argument for eliminating transactions with real estate from our sample. Regardless, if one finds that his or her sample size has more than enough transactions, one should consider rejecting those transactions that also included real estate.

THE FLORIDA EFFECT

Business Brokers of Florida (BBF) has been an enviable model of business broker cooperation. There are more business brokers in Florida and more businesses are sold through brokers there than just about every other state in the country. All brokers who are part of the association must report the transactional information from each of their sales to the BBF before they can receive their commission. Hence, BBF is able to collect a huge volume of transactional data, which finds its way to the various databases. Over the last ten years, 49% of Bizcomps' transactions, 39% of DealStats' transactions, and 28% of Valu-Source's transactions have come from BBF. Peercomps obtains most of its data from SBA banks and only has 14% of its transactions from the state of Florida. The concentration of Florida transactions is becoming so great that it is difficult to obtain samples for our valuations that do not have the appearance of a Florida bias.

However, the sheer number of Florida transactions is not the problem; the structure of the data is. It is not uncommon for some business brokers to inflate the cash flow in their business listings in order to attract buyers. More than likely this is an unintentional error, but many brokers are very liberal in identifying "add-backs" to cash flow thus inflating SDE. This tendency may be more prevalent in Florida due to the heightened competition among a very large number of brokers. Steve Mize, the owner of the Peercomps database, indicated in our

EXHIBIT 8.8 Concentration of Florida Transactions

	Bizcomps		ValuSource		DealStats		Peercomps	
	Florida	Non-FL	Florida	Non-FL	Florida	Non-FL	Florida	Non-FL
Cash Flow Multipliers	1.85	2.22	1.69	1.80	1.90	2.54	2.78	2.74
	Florida	Non-FL	Florida	Non-FL	Florida	Non-FL	Florida	Non-FL
Revenue Multipliers	0.47	0.47	0.41	0.40	0.42	0.47	0.66	0.66
	Florida	Non-FL	Florida	Non-FL	Florida	Non-FL	Florida	Non-FL
SDE%	25.6%	21.5%	25.4%	22.1%	22.8%	19.4%	24.5%	24.5%
All SIC codes and transactions with revenues between $100,000 to $4,000,000								
Excluding cash flow multipliers > 10 and less than 0.0 and all stock sales								

conversations that his primary incentive for starting Peercomps was Florida's data had excessively high profit margins resulting in low cash flow multiples. Exhibit 8.8 is an analysis of transactions found in each of the four databases. The transactions have been grouped into Florida transactions vs. non-Florida transactions.

All the Florida cash flow multipliers are lower than non-Florida sales, some by as much as 30% to 35%. Significant differences can be seen in three of the databases. The fourth database, Peercomps, obtains its transactional data from banks, not brokers. As such, its cash flow multipliers are relatively the same between Florida and non-Florida transactions.

The corresponding revenue multipliers, however, are reasonably similar regardless of location in all four databases. We can identify the possible source of the discrepancy in cash flow multipliers by observing the differences in the operating profit margins (SDE%) reported for Florida vs. non-Florida transactions. Florida brokers are calculating SDE for a given level of revenue much higher than all the other brokers in the country. Since Florida's reported SDE is higher, the resulting cash flow multipliers will be lower because SDE is the denominator of the multiplier ratio (price/SDE). Florida brokers appear to be reporting revenue and selling prices the same way as other brokers in the rest of the country as evidenced by their revenue multipliers being reasonably similar.

We can eliminate the hypothesis that Florida companies just generate more SDE than the rest of the country. Peercomps uses SBA banks rather than business brokers for its source of data. The cash flow multipliers reported by Peercomps are reasonably similar regardless of location. Peercomps' SDE% is also similar regardless of location. Hence, the only explanation left is that the Florida brokers' method of calculating SDE is clearly at odds with the rest of the country's.

TIMING OF A SALE

The transactions used for business valuations are often several years old. Most of us exposed to real estate appraisals on private residences have been told that proximity to the subject house and timing of the comparable's sale are critical to the valuation. Business valuations, however, are not calculated by looking at the actual selling price of the comparables. Instead, the subject company's financial ratios are compared with the ratios of the comparable businesses. As noted, some of these financial ratios have a tendency to be fairly consistent over time.

Secondly, small-business investors base their investment decisions primarily on a long-term view of the market. Unlike purchasing stock, where the holding period may be weeks or months, buyers of small businesses are often looking for career-length opportunities. Therefore, when comparing businesses that sold several years ago, the effects of recessions or bull markets on the revenue multiples of the business are somewhat minimalized. Again, by using financial ratio comparisons, the relationship between selling price and gross sales tends to be fairly stable over time. The time element that is so critical in real estate appraisals is not nearly as significant a factor in business appraisals.

The following research was discussed in the book *Understanding Business Valuation* by Gary Trugman:[6]

Raymond C. Miles, C.B.A., A.S.A., executive director of the Institute of Business Appraisers, published a paper entitled, "In Defense of Stale Comparables," in which Miles examined the almost 10,000 entries in the database, and demonstrated that most industries are unaffected by the date of the transaction when smaller businesses are involved. Miles performed a study that examined the multiples across various industries and time periods to see if, in fact, the multiples changed. The conclusion reached was that the multiples do not appear time-sensitive, since inflation affects not only the sales prices, but also the gross and net earnings of the business. Therefore, this information can be used to provide actual market data.

More recently, similar results were cited by Jack Sanders, the creator of BIZCOMPS database:[7]

Recently, the author [Jack Sanders] compared current study data with the data over ten years old. First the Gross Sales to Selling Price ratio was compared. In the current National Database that ratio was available in 6,748 out of 6,851 transactions. The arithmetic mean of this ratio was .46, while the median was .38. A similar analysis of 879 transactions out of 954 transactions older than ten years was made.

The arithmetic mean was .44 and the median was .37. The same analysis was made of the Seller's Discretionary Earnings (SDE) to Selling Price ratio. The

---

[6]Gary Trugman, *Understanding Business Valuation: A Practical Guide to Valuing Small to Medium Sized Businesses*, New York: American Institute of Certified Public Accountants, 1988, p. 150.
[7]Jack Sanders, "BIZCOMPS User Guide," Las Vegas, NV, 2004, p. 7.

arithmetic mean for the current study was 1.95 while the median was 1.8. In the over 10 year-old data, the arithmetic mean was 2.0 and the median was 1.8.

Granted, the two quotes go back many years, but that was the conventional thinking in the pre-recession days. In 2012, Gary Trugman updated his comments on Ray Miles' research, noting that transactions that were 15 years old were still valid. However, there were some industries where that thinking did not hold true.[8]

Recently, there have been some concerns raised by Toby Tatum that the recession has produced a significant amount of volatility in transactional multipliers during, and for several years after, the recession, which may skew one's results when employing the market approach.[9] To test that theory, I assembled a sample of transactions obtained from the DealStats database. The sample was filtered for all transactions between 1999 through 2018 with revenues under $3 million. Stock sale transactions were eliminated as were companies with breakeven cash flow (identified as transactions with cash flow multiples greater than 10.0) or negative cash flow.

The revenue multipliers and cash flow multipliers were calculated from each transaction's revenues, seller's discretionary earnings (SDE, or cash flow), and selling price. The data was sorted by the year in which the sale took place, and the resulting average value of the multipliers from each year was determined. The resulting sample of 16,731 transactions is listed in the table in Exhibit 8.9. The cash flow multipliers for the last twenty years are plotted in Exhibit 8.10 to illustrate the volatility the multipliers have experienced since the recession. From

---

[8]Gary Trugman, *Understanding Business Valuations: A Practical Guide to Valuing Small to Medium Sized Businesses*, 4th Edition, New York: American Institute of Certified Public Accountants, 2012, p. 353.
[9]Toby Tatum, "Analysis of Bizcomps Database: Past and Present, Business Appraisal Practice-Qtr IV," 2013, p. 19.

EXHIBIT 8.9   Multipliers by Year of Transaction.

Date Range		Count	Average Revenue Multipliers	Average Cash Flow Multipliers	Average SDE%
1-1-1999	12-31-1999	339	0.566	2.908	22.9%
1-1-2000	12-31-2000	414	0.580	3.144	21.9%
1-1-2001	12-31-2001	501	0.538	2.703	24.3%
1-1-2002	12-31-2002	594	0.558	2.835	24.7%
1-1-2003	12-31-2003	526	0.570	2.975	23.8%
1-1-2004	12-31-2004	765	0.576	3.014	23.7%
1-1-2005	12-31-2005	815	0.587	3.058	23.9%
1-1-2006	12-31-2006	839	0.588	3.045	23.7%
1-1-2007	12-31-2007	976	0.576	2.829	25.3%
1-1-2008	12-31-2008	1147	0.556	2.539	26.6%
1-1-2009	12-31-2009	788	0.561	2.437	27.9%
1-1-2010	12-31-2010	880	0.527	2.201	28.7%
1-1-2011	12-31-2011	855	0.552	2.423	26.9%
1-1-2012	12-31-2012	902	0.524	2.353	27.0%
1-1-2013	12-31-2013	965	0.551	2.411	26.6%
1-1-2014	12-31-2014	1065	0.572	2.489	27.3%
1-1-2015	12-31-2015	1127	0.548	2.539	25.5%
1-1-2016	12-31-2016	1250	0.553	2.542	25.4%
1-1-2017	12-31-2017	1019	0.580	2.664	24.7%
1-1-2018	12-31-2018	964	0.547	2.456	26.4%
	Averages	16,731	0.560	2.678	25.4%

Source: DealStats Database.

the peak in 2006, just before the start of the recession, cash flow multipliers declined 28% by 2010. If we were using the conventional medians to estimate the subject's appropriate multiplier and if our sample had a concentration of transactions that sold between 2010 to 2015, we would likely undervalue our subject.

Revenue multipliers, however, have remained fairly stable during the last twenty years. From Exhibit 8.11 we can see that revenue multipliers have fluctuated within a fairly tight range of less than plus or minus 10% from year to year. Even during the recession revenue multipliers held up remarkably well.

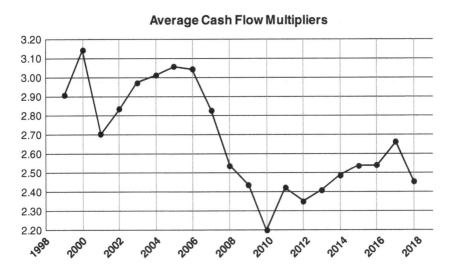

EXHIBIT 8.10 Average Cash Flow Multipliers 1999 to 2018

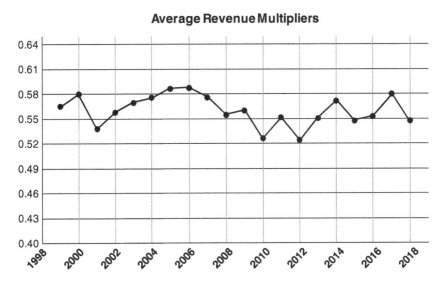

EXHIBIT 8.11 Average Revenue Multipliers 1999 to 2018

One's initial reaction is that appraisers should only use cash flow multipliers of transactions occurring during the most recent years to avoid undervaluing a business. Toby Tatum advanced an approach where an index would be created that reflects the current level of the multiplier with respect to its long-term average. The index would then be applied to the subject's calculated multiplier to adjust it to the current trend.[10]

Another alternative involves the use of regression analysis, which will allow us to use transactions over the last twenty years regardless of the level of multipliers of any one year.

As we learned in prior chapters, there is generally a moderate correlation between a company's operating profit margin (SDE%) and its corresponding cash flow multiplier. As such, we regressed the SDE% and the cash flow multipliers from Exhibit 8.8 for the last twenty years.

The results illustrated in Exhibit 8.12 were quite compelling. Visually we note that the dots representing the twenty years of multipliers were clustered tightly about the regression trend line. The regression produced a very high R^2 of 0.86, suggesting there is a strong correlation between a company's operating profit margin and the multiplier it earned, regardless of the effects of the recession.

To demonstrate, we take the above regression formula and plug in the 28.7% SDE% value from 2010, the low point for cash flow multipliers during the recession years:

$$y = -14.47x + 6.35$$

$$y = -14.47 \times 0.287 + 6.35 = 2.20$$

The actual multiplier for 2010 was 2.201.

The regression equation almost exactly predicted the average cash flow multiplier for 2010, the low point during the

---

[10]Toby Tatum, "Analysis of Bizcomps Database: Past and Present, Business Appraisal Practice-Qtr IV," 2013, p. 19.

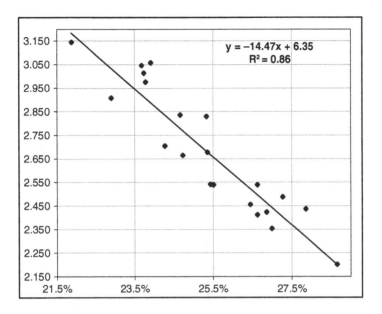

EXHIBIT 8.12 Regression of SDE Multipliers—1999 to 2018

recession. Taking the 23.7% SDE% for 2006, the peak year for multipliers prior to the recession, and applying the same regression formula we find:

$$y = -14.47x + 6.35$$

$$y = -14.47 \times 0.237 + 6.35 = 2.92$$

The actual multiplier for 2006 was 3.04.

The regression formula's 2.92 prediction for the peak year was only 4% less than the 3.04 actual value.

Clearly the regression methodology can accurately calculate multipliers regardless of the age of the transaction; medians cannot.

If we look closely at the operating profit margins (SDE%) over the last twenty years, we note that during the recession years profit margins actually increased. That seems to be counterintuitive. However, as we learned in the prior chapters, as a company's SDE% profit margin increased, its cash flow multipliers decreased, which is what happened during the recession.

I was a business broker before, during, and after the recession, and I witnessed firsthand one reason for this apparent anomaly. Prior to the recession small-business owners were living the good life. Profits were abundant. The owners played golf twice a week. They could afford to hire a manager so that they wouldn't have to work more than 30 hours a week. When the recession hit, the owners immediately did everything they could to protect their lifestyles. They jumped back into the trenches, worked 60-hour weeks, cut every expense, and fired the manager. From the example below, we observe that sales may have declined 25% by the depths of the recession, but the owner's efforts to protect his lifestyle held profits to a 17% decrease. Sales and cash flow both declined. However, the end result was that the company's SDE% increased from 30.0% in 2006 to 33.0% in 2010.

2006	2010		Decline
Sales	$2,000,000	$1,500,000	–25.0%
SDE	$600,000	$500,000	–17%
SDE%	30.0%	33.3%	

Had the owner sold his business in 2006, he could have earned $600,000 × 3.04 = $1,824,000. By 2010 the business was only worth $500,000 × 2.2 = $1,100,000—a higher profit margin but a lower multiplier.

I must offer a modest disclaimer for the events that occurred during the recession as I described them. I found the highest correlation between profit margins and cash flow multipliers in companies with less than $3 million in revenue. The significance all but disappeared when analyzing companies over $3 million in revenue. I believe the reason is that the small business owners have far more control over the day-to-day decision making when it comes to deciding how and when to cut expenses. Hence, those owners were able to protect profit levels better. Larger companies have many layers of bureaucracy, multiple owners, and often have board members who have different agendas than the prime owner. Thus, expenses often did not get cut as deeply as a small business owner could make.

CHAPTER 9

Regression 2.0

The regression template and all the discussion on the regression methodology thus far has been oriented toward the basic procedure I have used for many years with great results. In the last few years I decided to take it up a notch and fine-tune the process. The four regression methodologies discussed in this book all work on the assumption that a transaction in a sample that was more than one standard error from the trend line would be considered an outlier. The first-level regression we ran would identify the outliers and the second-level regression with the outliers removed produced the trendline formula used to calculate the multipliers for the subject.

If you were able to wrap your mind around all that math and statistics, you may be ready for the advanced course—Regression 2.0. If the fog hasn't lifted yet, go to the next chapter, and bypass this one.

In this chapter we will explore three additions to the regression methodology designed to fine-tune the final conclusion of value:

1. Rather than two levels of regressions, we will consider running up to four regressions with outliers being removed at each successive level. By removing more transactions that are considered outliers, R^2 will increase, and the resulting regression may be a more accurate indication of where the market is.

2. In our original two-level regression methodology introduced in Chapter 3, we arbitrarily chose the break point for determining outliers at 1.0 times the standard error of the regression. At one standard error we would expect 16% of our sample of transactions would fall above that value and 16% would fall below it. The remaining 68% of the sample would be considered mainstream transactions that reflect where the market is.

Rather than running two regressions using a standard error of 1.0, we will run four regressions using 1.1 times the standard error to identify the outliers at each level. Then we will repeat the process using 1.2 times the standard error, all the way up to 1.8 times the standard error.

By widening the standard error range at each successive regression level, we will be taking smaller slices out of the sample. The desired outcome would be that only the most flawed outliers are removed, leaving a larger percentage of transactions in the sample, yet R^2 still improves.

For example, at 1.5 times the standard error, only 6.7% of the transactions in the sample will fall above the break point and 6.7% will fall below the break point. The remaining 86.6% of the sample will be considered acceptable in determining the appropriate multipliers for the subject. Thus, by the time we reach the third- or fourth-level regression we may obtain a higher R^2 with fewer outliers removed from the sample.

If you did the math quickly in your head, for each sample I analyze, I run four regressions with nine different standard error break points, or 36 regressions in all. Fortunately, as will be demonstrated in the next two chapters, Excel can perform this Herculean feat in seconds. Each of the 36 regressions is given a rating based on its R^2 and the number of outliers that were removed. The sample that produced the highest R^2 with the fewest outliers removed is selected to calculate the multipliers.

3. The multiple variable regression uses up to four independent variables in the resulting formula. The regression also provides us with an R^2, which measures the accuracy of the formula. However, a high R^2 does not tell us if each of the four independent variable's coefficients contributed equally in predicting the overall value. The Excel regression utility calculates P-values for each of the four variables that indicate the level of accuracy of each variable. This information is used to fine-tune our selection process of the best sample to estimate the subject's value.

FOUR LEVELS OF REGRESSIONS

The template introduced in the last chapter ran just two regressions. The first regression identified the outliers in the sample introduced in Exhibit 2.1, and the second regression without the outliers produced the formula used to calculate the multipliers. Exhibit 9.1 below illustrates the results of the first-level regression. The R^2 was an unimpressive 0.37. The regression identified eight transactions as outliers.

When the eight outliers are removed and the second-level regression is run, we find the R^2 increased significantly to 0.71. However, this second-level regression identified another six transactions that were considered outliers in the smaller sample of 16 transactions. The third-level regression removed those six transactions, raising the R^2 to 0.89. Four more outliers are identified in the third-level regression. The fourth-level regression produced a very impressive 0.95 R^2. However, there were only six transactions remaining in the sample out of the 24 we started with.

It is interesting to note that the remaining six transactions lined up so tightly along the regression line. As such, six transactions out of the 24 were very predictable. Ideally however, we would like to end up with a majority of the transactions in our sample for the final-level regression (as much as 2/3 of the

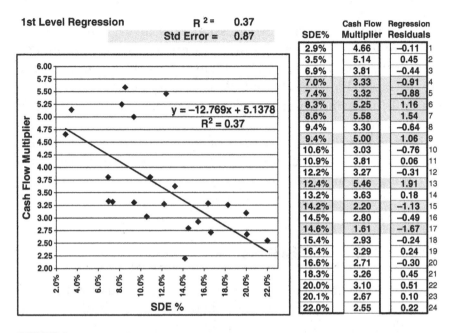

EXHIBIT 9.1　First-Level Regression

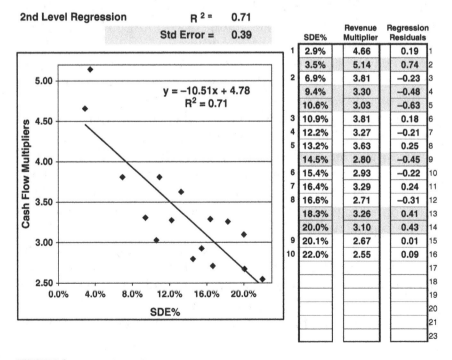

EXHIBIT 9.2　Second-Level Regression

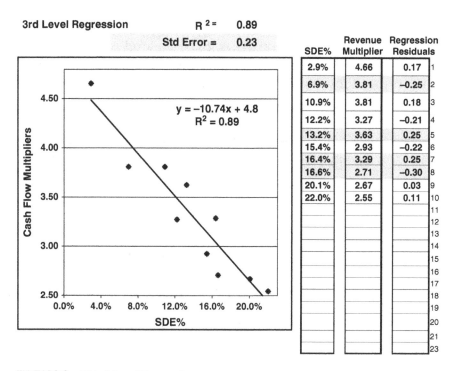

3rd Level Regression R² = 0.89

Std Error = 0.23

SDE%	Revenue Multiplier	Regression Residuals	
2.9%	4.66	0.17	1
6.9%	3.81	−0.25	2
10.9%	3.81	0.18	3
12.2%	3.27	−0.21	4
13.2%	3.63	0.25	5
15.4%	2.93	−0.22	6
16.4%	3.29	0.25	7
16.6%	2.71	−0.30	8
20.1%	2.67	0.03	9
22.0%	2.55	0.11	10

$y = -10.74x + 4.8$
$R^2 = 0.89$

EXHIBIT 9.3 Third-Level Regression

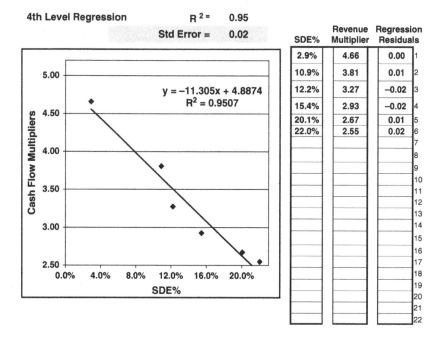

4th Level Regression R² = 0.95

Std Error = 0.02

SDE%	Revenue Multiplier	Regression Residuals	
2.9%	4.66	0.00	1
10.9%	3.81	0.01	2
12.2%	3.27	−0.02	3
15.4%	2.93	−0.02	4
20.1%	2.67	0.01	5
22.0%	2.55	0.02	6

$y = -11.305x + 4.8874$
$R^2 = 0.9507$

EXHIBIT 9.4 Fourth-Level Regression

sample). The objective is to identify the appropriate multipliers exhibited in the subject's market given its level of profitability. Even though the sample of six were so predictable, six out of 24 is rather thin to gauge where the market is.

I use a simple formula to rate each level of the regressions.

O = The number of outliers that were removed.

S = The number of transactions in the original sample.

$$R2R = \frac{(S - O) \times R^2}{S}$$

This rating factor (which I call R2R) is basically looking for the regression that has the highest R^2 with the fewest outliers removed.

The R2R for each of the four previous regressions is:

Level #1 = (24 − 0) ÷ 24 × 0.37 = 0.37
Level #2 = (24 − 8) ÷ 24 × 0.71 = 0.47
Level #3 = (24 − 14) ÷ 24 × 0.89 = 0.37
Level #4 = (24 − 18) ÷ 24 × 0.95 = 0.24

Level#2 is found to be the best R2R regression. It achieved a moderately high R^2 factor with the least number of outliers removed from the sample.

ADJUSTING THE STANDARD ERROR BREAK POINT

Adjusting the standard error break point is an extension of the four-level regression technique. This variation is very labor intensive unless you are able to create macros in Excel to perform the 36 regressions.

The majority of the time the four-level regression using one standard error as the break point for identifying outliers produces reasonable results. As such, deciding not to venture into adjusting the standard error will not necessarily sacrifice accuracy. However, looking at the sample of transactions from 36 different directions can sometimes reveal idiosyncrasies caused by one or two transactions.

Following is a similar four-level regression method with the same sample as in Exhibits 9.1 to 9.4. The difference is the 0.87 standard error is multiplied by 1.1 and the resulting 0.96 value becomes the new break point of the residuals from each regression.

When increasing the breakpoint to just 1.1 times the standard error you will notice that the number of outliers identified in the first level was only six compared to eight when using one standard error. The second-level regression at $1.0 \times$ the standard error found 16 transactions and produced an R^2 of 0.71, whereas the regression using a 1.1 breakpoint produced an R^2 of only 0.61. However, it was on a larger sample of 18.

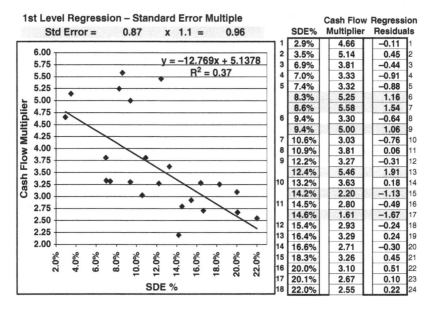

EXHIBIT 9.5   First-Level Regression – Standard Error × 1.1

2nd Level Regression – Standard Error Multiple

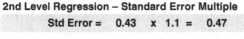

SDE%	Cash Flow Multiplier	Regression Residuals	
2.9%	4.66	0.40	1
3.5%	5.14	0.94	2
6.9%	3.81	−0.08	3
7.0%	3.33	−0.55	4
7.4%	3.32	−0.53	5
9.4%	3.30	−0.36	6
10.6%	3.03	−0.53	7
10.9%	3.81	0.28	8
12.2%	3.27	−0.13	9
13.2%	3.63	0.32	10
14.5%	2.80	−0.40	11
15.4%	2.93	−0.18	12
16.4%	3.29	0.27	13
16.6%	2.71	−0.29	14
18.3%	3.26	0.41	15
20.0%	3.10	0.40	16
20.1%	2.67	−0.01	17
22.0%	2.55	0.04	18
			19
			20
			21
			22
			23

EXHIBIT 9.6   Second-Level Regression – Standard Error × 1.1

3rd Level Regression – Standard Error Multiple

Std Error = 0.308 x 1.1 = 0.339

$y = -9.02 + 4.55$
$R^2 = 0.73$

SDE%	Cash Flow Multiplier	Regression Residuals	
2.9%	4.66	0.37	1
6.9%	3.81	−0.12	2
9.4%	3.30	−0.40	3
10.9%	3.81	0.24	4
12.2%	3.27	−0.18	5
13.2%	3.63	0.27	6
14.5%	2.80	−0.45	7
15.4%	2.93	−0.23	8
16.4%	3.29	0.21	9
16.6%	2.71	−0.34	10
18.3%	3.26	0.35	11
20.0%	3.10	0.35	12
20.1%	2.67	−0.07	13
22.0%	2.55	−0.02	14
			15
			16
			17
			18
			19
			20
			21
			22
			23

EXHIBIT 9.7   Third-Level Regression – Standard Error × 1.1

By the time we reach the 4th-level regression, there are eight transactions remaining and the R^2 increases to 0.84. When we used the 1.0 × the standard error break point, we had a slightly higher R^2 but only six transactions remaining. The R2R rating for the 1.1 break point was 0.279 compared to the 0.238 rating of the 1.0 break point. The R2R rating for the 1.1 break point was higher; however, the remaining sample was still too small to be relevant.

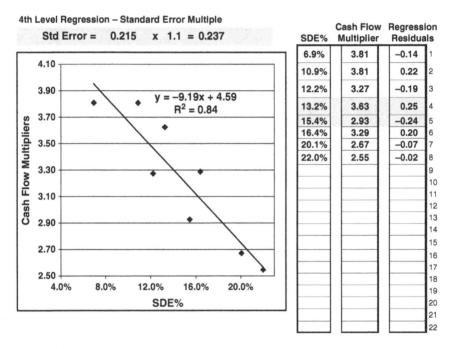

4th Level Regression – Standard Error Multiple

Std Error = 0.215   x 1.1 = 0.237

y = −9.19x + 4.59
R^2 = 0.84

SDE%	Cash Flow Multiplier	Regression Residuals	
6.9%	3.81	−0.14	1
10.9%	3.81	0.22	2
12.2%	3.27	−0.19	3
13.2%	3.63	0.25	4
15.4%	2.93	−0.24	5
16.4%	3.29	0.20	6
20.1%	2.67	−0.07	7
22.0%	2.55	−0.02	8
			9
			10
			11
			12
			13
			14
			15
			16
			17
			18
			19
			20
			21
			22

EXHIBIT 9.8 Fourth-Level Regression – Standard Error × 1.1

The following table increases the standard error adjustment in increments of 0.1 from 1.0 × the standard error to 1.8 × the standard error. Using our R2R formula as a selection criterion, the second-level regression of the 1.0 break point earned a 47.7 R2R rating and the second-level regression of the 1.1 break point earned a 46.3 rating, basically a toss-up. Coincidentally, duplicate regressions with 46.3 R2R ratings were found in regression level #2–1.2 break point, level #3–1.4 break point, level #3–1.5 break point, level #3–1.6 break point, and level #3–1.7 break point.

EXHIBIT 9.9 Regressions with Outliers Removed at 1.1 to 1.8 Times Standard Error

Std Er	Regression Level ↓	Obs.	Outliers	R2R Rating	R2	Multiplier
1.0	#2	16	8	0.477	0.715	2.190
	#3	10	14	0.370	0.887	2.116
	#4	6	18	0.238	0.951	2.063
1.1	#2	18	6	0.463	0.617	2.234
	#3	14	10	0.425	0.729	2.297
	#4	8	16	0.279	0.837	2.293
1.2	#2	18	6	0.463	0.617	2.234
	#3	14	10	0.425	0.729	2.297
	#4	11	13	0.317	0.691	2.418
1.3	#2	20	4	0.426	0.511	2.121
	#3	17	7	0.409	0.577	2.407
	#4	16	8	0.300	0.450	2.588
1.4	#2	21	3	0.432	0.493	2.064
	#3	18	6	0.463	0.617	2.234
	#4	17	7	0.409	0.577	2.407
1.5	#2	21	3	0.432	0.493	2.064
	#3	18	6	0.463	0.617	2.234
	#4	17	7	0.409	0.577	2.407
1.6	#2	21	3	0.432	0.493	2.064
	#3	18	6	0.463	0.617	2.234
	#4	17	7	0.409	0.577	2.407
1.7	#2	21	3	0.432	0.493	2.064
	#3	18	6	0.463	0.617	2.234
	#4	17	7	0.409	0.577	2.407
1.8	#2	22	2	0.428	0.467	2.012
	#3	21	3	0.432	0.493	2.064
	#4	19	5	0.444	0.561	2.146
Averages w/ < 33% Outliers				0.43	0.56	2.23

The R2R rating for level #2–1.0 and level #2–1.1 are the highest ratings out of the 36 regressions. The cash flow multiplier calculated by the 1.1 regression was slightly higher than the multiplier from the 1.0 regression. The regressions that had less than 1/3 of the transactions removed as outliers are better indicators of where the market is because they included a larger percentage of the sample's transactions in the analysis. The average of the samples with less than eight outliers removed was 2.23. Consequently, out of the 36 regressions level #2–1.1 appears to be the best choice with the second highest rating and a multiplier of 2.234.

MULTIPLE VARIABLE REGRESSION STATISTICS

The multiple variable regression methodology explored in prior chapters uses up to four variables to predict the subject's overall value. Generally, up to four variables can be extracted from the various transactional databases: revenue, cash flow (SDE), inventory, and fixed assets. These are the independent variables in the regression equation that are used to predict the dependent variable—the selling price of a business. We will use the same approach discussed previously for the single-variable regressions in which we test four levels of regressions at nine different multiples of the standard error. After running all 36 regressions, which one do we select as the best choice to value our subject?

After running a regression, Excel's regression utility gives a printout that calculates various statistical measures that will help us select the best sample to determine the value of our subject. We have already noted that the R^2 is a measure of the accuracy of the regression formula. However, we cannot assume that each of the four independent variables contributed equally to the final value. Ordinarily this wouldn't be a big issue because, after all, a high R^2 suggests that the end result of the regression is accurate. What more do we need?

First of all, just as in the case of the single-variable regressions discussed above, by the time we reach the third- or fourth-level regression we often find that the majority of the transactions have often been removed from the sample. The remaining transactions will usually produce a moderately high R^2. However, with less than two-thirds of the transactions left in the sample, are we really getting a good estimate of where the market is? Consequently, we will use the same R2R rating methodology for the multiple variable regression as we did with the single-variable regressions. But with four independent variables in the methodology, the R2R rating may not point out the best regression.

In different valuation assignments we might find that our subject had much higher-than-average values for cash flow, inventory, or fixtures and equipment. If the subject's value for inventory was the variable in question, we would want the regression formula to have properly weighted inventory in the conclusion of value. If a particular sample did not provide us with that assurance, the regression formula may produce skewed results for our high-inventory subject even though the regression formula had an overall R2R rating that was very high.

Exhibit 9.10 below is a typical printout of Excel's regression data:

In the lower left corner, we find the coefficients for the four independent variables used in the regression formula to predict the dependent variable, the selling price. The five coefficients resulted in the following formula:

$$\text{Selling Price} = .1022 \times \text{Revenue} + 3.93 \times \text{SDE} - 1.19$$
$$\times \text{Inventory} + .334 \times \text{Fixtures} - \$738{,}640$$

Just to the right of those five coefficients is the standard error calculated for each of them. This is different than the standard error for the whole equation. With a standard error produced on each variable we can identify which ones were poor predictors for that variable's value. To the right of the standard error column is the t-Stat column. The t Stat is the independent

EXHIBIT 9.10   P and T Statistics from Excel's Regression Printout

SUMMARY OUTPUT								
Regression Statistics								
Multiple R	0.95							
R Squared	0.90							
Adjusted R Squared	0.88							
Standard Error	363,056							
Observations	23							

ANOVA						
	df	*SS*	*MS*	*F*	*Significance F*	
Regression	4	2.1879E+13	5.4697E+12	41.497297	7.49E-09	
Residual	18	2.3726E+12	1.3181E+11			
Total	22	2.4252E+13				

	Coefficient	*Standard Error*	*t Stat*	*P-Value*	*Lower 95%*	*Upper 95%*	*Lower 95.0%*	*Upper 95.0%*
Intercept	−738,640	279,458	−2.64311	0.017	−1,325,760	−151,520	−1,325,760	−151,520
Revenues	0.102156	0.120	0.84969	0.407	−0.1504	0.3547	−0.1504	0.3547
SDE	3.93356	0.384	10.24329	0.000	3.1268	4.7403	3.1268	4.7403
Inventory	−1.19358	0.573	−2.08141	0.052	−2.3983	0.0112	−2.3983	0.0112
Fixtures	0.334101	0.382	0.87529	0.393	−0.4678	1.1360	−0.4678	1.1360

variable's coefficient divided by its standard error. The smaller the standard error relative to the value of the corresponding coefficient, the larger the resulting t Stat. Hence, we note the coefficient for SDE was 3.93 and its standard error was only 0.38. The small standard error in the denominator of the t Stat resulted in a very high value of 10.24. As such, a high t Stat value suggests that there was a very tight grouping of that variable's calculated values about its regression trend line. In other words, the higher the t Stat, the more accurate the regression coefficient predicted that variable's contribution to the total value of the business.

The t Stat and the P-value are numerically linked. The higher the t Stat, the lower the P-value. The P-values test the hypothesis that there is no correlation between the independent variable in the sample and the values observed in the larger population of all businesses. The closer the P-value is to zero, the more it suggests that we can reject the null hypothesis that there is no correlation. In plain English, a low P-value suggests that there *is* a correlation between the independent variable and the resulting value of all businesses (i.e., the lower the value, the stronger the relationship).

For the purposes of rating all our samples, we will consider anything less than a 0.50 P-value as an indication that the independent variable produced a reasonable correlation to the final value of the business.

From the previous section we introduced the R2R rating factor based on the number of outliers removed from a sample and the resulting R^2. ($R^2 \times$ remaining observations ÷ total transactions.) The sample with the highest R^2 and the least number of outliers removed was accorded the highest R2R rating and was considered our best choice of samples to value the subject business.

For the multiple variable regression, we now can introduce a second rating element, the P-values earned by each of the four independent variables. The five columns on the right side of Exhibit 9.11 below contain the P-values for each independent variable. To the left of those five columns is the total of the five P-values for each transaction. The sample with the lowest total P-value most likely has the best rating of the combined variables. Hence, we are looking for a sample with the highest R2R rating and the lowest total P-values.

Dividing each sample's total P-value by its R2R rating gives us a means to rate a particular sample (which I call the overall rating). The ratio that produces the lowest overall rating is our best choice of samples. It is the sample whose transactions closely align with each other (as measured by R^2) and whose individual independent variables are statistically relevant. Hence, that sample is our best choice to accurately value our subject business.

In Exhibit 9.11, level #2–1.2 had the lowest overall rating of 0.40. That sample's P-value for inventory was 0.128 and the P-value for fixtures was 0.02. As such, it was the best

EXHIBIT 9.11 Selecting a Sample with the Highest Overall Rating

Std Err Mult	Reg Level	Obs.	Outliers	R2R Rating	R²	Value	Overall Rating P-Val ÷ R2R	Total P-Val	P-Val Sales	P-Val CF	P-Val Inv	P-Val FF&E	P-Val Interc
1.0	2	17	6	0.722	0.98	837,772	1.064	0.769	0.698	0.000	0.027	0.042	0.002
1.0	3	14	9	0.605	0.99	950,152	*n/a	0.506	0.492	0.000	0.013	0.001	0.000
1.0	4	10	13	0.434	1.00	919,592	*n/a	0.093	0.090	0.000	0.002	0.001	0.000
1.1	2	18	5	0.759	0.97	795,215	0.788	0.599	0.405	0.000	0.095	0.098	0.001
1.1	3	15	8	0.646	0.99	910,438	*n/a	0.324	0.243	0.000	0.077	0.004	0.000
1.1	4	13	10	0.563	1.00	952,441	*n/a	0.109	0.101	0.000	0.007	0.001	0.000
1.2	2	20	3	0.837	0.96	819,447	0.400	0.334	0.186	0.000	0.128	0.020	0.000
1.2	3	18	5	0.766	0.98	919,083	0.930	0.713	0.310	0.000	0.400	0.002	0.000
1.2	4	14	9	0.603	0.99	902,987	*n/a	0.271	0.170	0.000	0.097	0.004	0.000
1.3	2	20	3	0.837	0.96	819,447	0.400	0.334	0.186	0.000	0.128	0.020	0.000
1.3	3	19	4	0.806	0.98	889,664	1.122	0.904	0.195	0.000	0.704	0.004	0.000
1.3	4	18	5	0.766	0.98	875,090	1.119	0.857	0.110	0.000	0.745	0.002	0.000
1.4	2	21	2	0.869	0.95	861,331	0.700	0.609	0.330	0.000	0.239	0.038	0.001
1.4	3	19	4	0.806	0.98	889,664	1.122	0.904	0.195	0.000	0.704	0.004	0.000
1.4	4	19	4	0.806	0.98	889,664	1.122	0.904	0.195	0.000	0.704	0.004	0.000
1.5	2	21	2	0.869	0.95	861,331	0.700	0.609	0.330	0.000	0.239	0.038	0.001
1.5	3	19	4	0.806	0.98	889,664	1.122	0.904	0.195	0.000	0.704	0.004	0.000
1.5	4	19	4	0.806	0.98	889,664	1.122	0.904	0.195	0.000	0.704	0.004	0.000
1.6	2	21	2	0.869	0.95	861,331	0.700	0.609	0.330	0.000	0.239	0.038	0.001
1.6	3	19	4	0.806	0.98	889,664	1.122	0.904	0.195	0.000	0.704	0.004	0.000
1.6	4	19	4	0.806	0.98	889,664	1.122	0.904	0.195	0.000	0.704	0.004	0.000
1.7	2	21	2	0.869	0.95	861,331	0.700	0.609	0.330	0.000	0.239	0.038	0.001
1.7	3	19	4	0.806	0.98	889,664	1.122	0.904	0.195	0.000	0.704	0.004	0.000
1.7	4	19	4	0.806	0.98	889,664	1.122	0.904	0.195	0.000	0.704	0.004	0.000
1.8	2	22	1	0.885	0.93	835,793	0.601	0.532	0.357	0.000	0.065	0.102	0.008
1.8	3	21	2	0.869	0.95	861,331	0.700	0.609	0.330	0.000	0.239	0.038	0.001
1.8	4	20	3	0.841	0.97	932,321	1.617	1.360	0.365	0.000	0.986	0.009	0.000
			Average Values =	0.773	0.972	880,867							

*n/a = samples rejected due to high % of outliers removed

119

choice to value our subject. Given the subject's high level of fixtures and inventory, we would want those two individual independent variables to have low P-values. So, for example, if level #3–1.3 were the lowest overall rating, its P-value for inventory was 0.704. Consequently, the regression formula for that sample may not have properly valued the inventory component even though its overall rating was high. As such, that sample may not have been a good choice to value our subject.

It is important that consideration should be given to the individual P-values for each coefficient. For the final checkpoint we noted that the subject had a moderately higher level of inventory than the average company in the sample. Hence, we want to make sure that the P-value for the inventory coefficient on the sample we chose had a value less than 0.50. If the value exceeds 0.50, the coefficient for inventory may not be accurate. Consequently, the best choice of the regressions would be the one with the *next best* overall rating where the P-value for inventory was less than 0.50.

CHAPTER 10

Using Excel's Regression Utility

One important consideration when preparing a valuation is that the data presented should be replicable. Appraisers hate black-box numbers that appear out of nowhere, for which the reader cannot calculate. Consequently, if one decides to use the data and charts from the regression template in his or her own valuation report, one may wish to show more of the regression data that Excel generates.

This chapter will take the reader through all the steps necessary to employ Excel's regression utility. The first step is to "enable," that is, to install the regression utility in one's computer. Regardless of whether Excel was pre-installed on your computer or you downloaded the program from a CD or you use the online version, the regression utility is not pre-installed. It is a fairly simple process, which only has to be done once on every computer in which you intend to use the regression utility.

INSTALLING EXCEL'S REGRESSION

The screen shots for the following steps are illustrated on the next page.

Step #1—Boot up a blank worksheet in Excel. In the upper-left corner you must click on "File" on the menu ribbon.

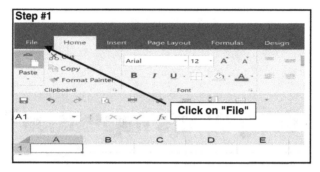

EXHIBIT 10.1
Source: Used with permission from Microsoft Corporation

Step #2—The "Open" window will pop up. Click on "Options" at the bottom of the menu screen.

EXHIBIT 10.2
Source: Used with
permission from
Microsoft Corporation

Step #3—At the bottom of the Options window that pops up next, click on the "Add-ins" menu.

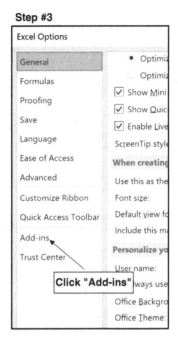

EXHIBIT 10.3
Source: Used with permission
from Microsoft Corporation

Step #4—After clicking on "Add-ins," the "Option" window will display a "Go . . ." button at the bottom of the screen. Click "Go . . . ."

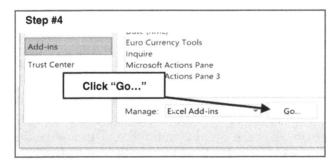

EXHIBIT 10.4

Step #5—No surprise here. Another window pops up.

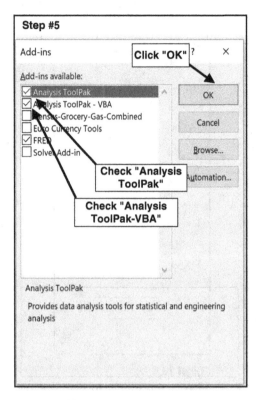

EXHIBIT 10.5
Source: Used with permission from Microsoft
Corporation

In Exhibit 10.5 check off the boxes entitled "Analysis Tool-Pak" and "Analysis ToolPak-VBA." Then click on the "OK" button, and you are done. The window reverts back to the blank worksheet.

I know this process was cumbersome, but fortunately you only need to do this once. But you must also do it once on every computer where you intend to use the regression utility.

Once the installation is complete, you will notice that a new menu option appears on the main Excel menu ribbon called "Data." Now you are ready to access the regression utility. And, to no one's surprise, there are a few more buttons to click to get you there.

Click on "Data," then "Data Analysis," and then scroll down on the Data Analysis window to "Regression."

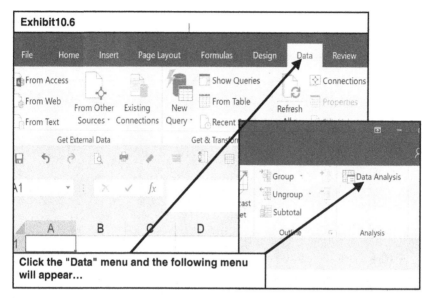

EXHIBIT 10.6
Source: Used with permission from Microsoft Corporation

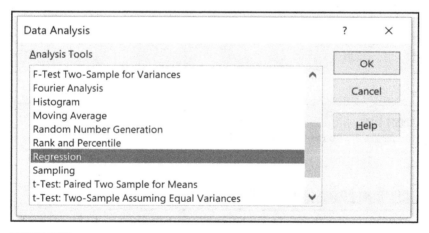

EXHIBIT 10.7
Source: Used with permission from Microsoft Corporation

I know it was three more clicks, but it gets easier after you do it a few thousand times like I have. After these three clicks we now are presented with the following regression window.

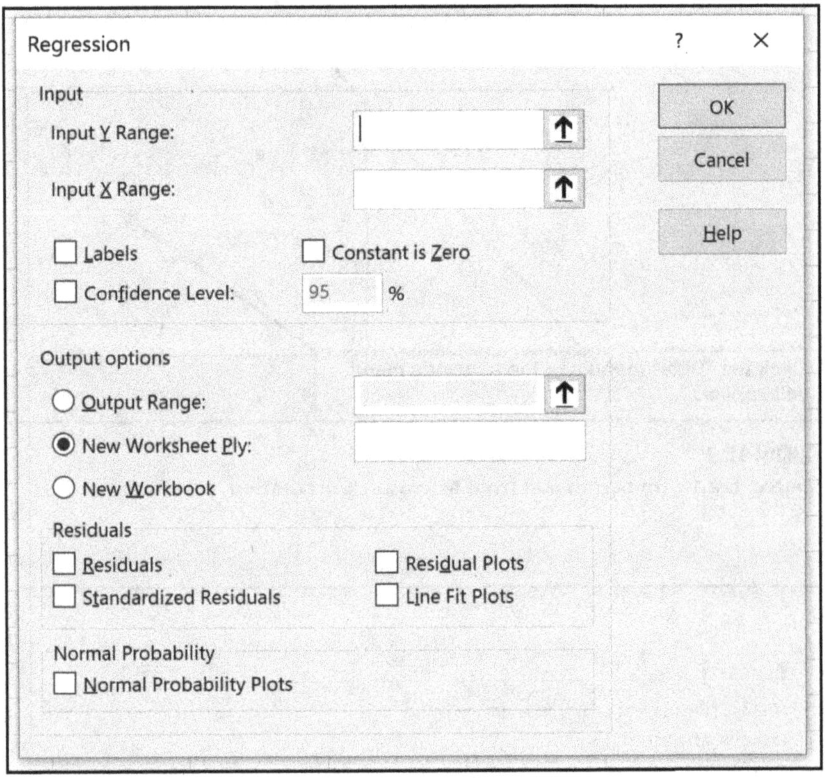

EXHIBIT 10.8 Regression Window
Source: Used with permission from Microsoft Corporation

EXCEL'S REGRESSION UTILITY

The data that one needs to enter in the above fields is best described by running the regression for the original sample of 24 transactions that was introduced in Chapter 2. In chapter 4 we presented the findings of the regression on the cash flow multipliers of that sample of 24 transactions. The results of the first-level regression were graphed in Exhibit 4.3. That regression produced an R^2 of 0.37 and the following formula for the trend line:

$$Y = -12.77x + 5.13$$

The initial setup for that regression is illustrated in Exhibit 10.9.

The first data field in the regression window is "Input Y range." The Y variables are the dependent variables that we are trying to predict, in this case, cash flow multipliers. The data entered in this field is the location of the array or column of data that contains the Y variables of the 24 transactions in the sample. In the Exhibit 10.9, the cash flow multiplier variables are in the array described as $H$5:$H$28, which is in cell H5 through cell H28.

The "Input X range" is the location of the X variables. The X variables are the 24 transactions' SDE%, which are the independent variables being used to predict the cash flow multipliers. The location of this data is the array $F$5:$F$28.

In regression's linear equation, $y = mx + b$; the X variables (SDE%) are always graphed on the horizontal, or X, axis. The Y variables (the multiplier we are trying to predict) are always graphed on the vertical, or Y, axis. If you can never remember which way the two axes go, just remember "Y to the sky and X to the desk." (I thank my algebra teacher for that one.)

The next data field to enter is the "Output Range." The regression printout is nine columns wide and as many as 70 rows deep. If there is any other data on your worksheet that is in the regression's path, it will be erased. Hence, first make sure the printout is well out of the way of anything else on the worksheet. The "Output Range" starts at the very upper-left corner of the data printout. In the exhibit 10.9, I chose cell $L$1 as the starting point. Hence, the regression printout will cover cells L1 to U1 wide and from L1 to L70 deep.

Under the "Residuals" section we want to check the "Residuals" box. We will need the residual information to determine which transactions will be identified as outliers (i.e., when the residual is greater than the standard error).

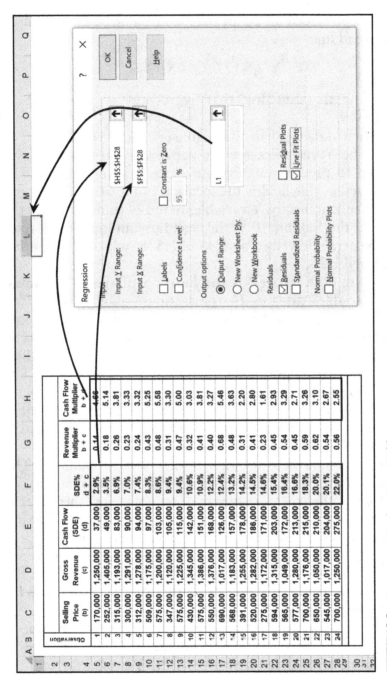

EXHIBIT 10.9 Regression Window Data Fields

Source: Used with permission from Microsoft Corporation

Lastly, we should check off the box labeled "Line Fit Plots." This optional field will create the charts that you have seen throughout this book. More on creating the regression graphs will be discussed later in this chapter in the "Production Value of Excel" section.

Exhibit 10.10 is a printout of the report that is generated with each regression. (I eliminated a few columns of data to the right of the P-values due to space limitations.) The data in the printout is also carried out to five or six decimal places. I shortened them to two decimal places for easier reading. The locations of the various data that we have discussed throughout this book are indicated by the arrows. This one printout from the regression utility gives us the R^2, the standard error, the t Stat for each coefficient, the P-value for each coefficient, the coefficients used in the linear equation, and the residuals for each of the 24 transactions. At the top of this printout we note that the standard error was 0.87. We can compare this number to the absolute value of each of the 24 residuals (i.e., ignore the minus sign). A residual that is greater than the standard error is considered an outlier. Hence, observation #4, #5, #6, #7, #9, #13, #15, and #17 are considered outliers.

MULTIPLE VARIABLE REGRESSIONS

The information and exhibits are for single variable regressions. The multiple variable regressions are slightly different, but the differences are important to note. The multiple variable sample that we introduced in Chapter 6 (Exhibit 6.2), is shown in Exhibit 10.11 with the regression utility filled out and ready to run.

The "Input Y Range" in this example is the selling price of the transactions in the sample rather than the revenue or cash flow multiplier. The location of the selling price data is in array $C$4:$C$26. The "Input X Range" includes each transaction's revenue, cash flow, inventory, and fixtures and

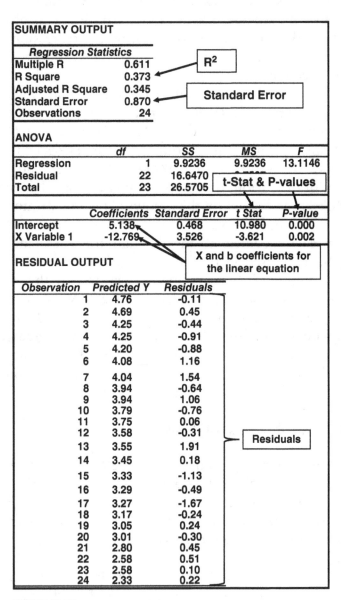

SUMMARY OUTPUT

Regression Statistics	
Multiple R	0.611
R Square	0.373
Adjusted R Square	0.345
Standard Error	0.870
Observations	24

R^2

Standard Error

ANOVA

	df	SS	MS	F
Regression	1	9.9236	9.9236	13.1146
Residual	22	16.6470		
Total	23	26.5705		

t-Stat & P-values

	Coefficients	Standard Error	t Stat	P-value
Intercept	5.138	0.468	10.980	0.000
X Variable 1	-12.769	3.526	-3.621	0.002

RESIDUAL OUTPUT

X and b coefficients for the linear equation

Observation	Predicted Y	Residuals
1	4.76	-0.11
2	4.69	0.45
3	4.25	-0.44
4	4.25	-0.91
5	4.20	-0.88
6	4.08	1.16
7	4.04	1.54
8	3.94	-0.64
9	3.94	1.06
10	3.79	-0.76
11	3.75	0.06
12	3.58	-0.31
13	3.55	1.91
14	3.45	0.18
15	3.33	-1.13
16	3.29	-0.49
17	3.27	-1.67
18	3.17	-0.24
19	3.05	0.24
20	3.01	-0.30
21	2.80	0.45
22	2.58	0.51
23	2.58	0.10
24	2.33	0.22

Residuals

EXHIBIT 10.10　Regression Printout

	Price	Revenues	SDE	Inventory	Fixtures
1	4,50,000	29,71,358	2,33,651	1,00,000	1,00,000
2	9,40,000	37,05,000	4,04,000	40,000	3,09,000
3	9,90,000	35,00,000	4,27,841	1,87,510	2,12,489
4	5,30,183	18,01,092	2,54,321	50,000	3,50,000
5	7,66,959	22,33,258	3,31,424	3,61,630	4,26,657
6	13,95,000	29,30,376	4,96,820	40,947	48,310
7	22,08,692	36,20,708	6,67,675	2,69,471	3,17,928
8	15,10,022	23,86,283	4,58,137	1,10,022	6,00,000
9	13,00,000	19,00,000	3,85,000	1,83,501	2,16,498
10	15,66,925	28,01,382	6,68,522	5,12,393	6,04,531
11	9,25,000	15,28,734	3,72,403	38,490	45,412
12	35,00,000	34,04,875	8,81,344	1,23,000	9,69,482
13	17,00,000	25,33,000	6,93,000	1,26,000	50,000
14	11,50,000	17,20,000	4,80,000	30,000	3,14,000
15	26,00,000	29,00,000	8,14,000	5,50,504	6,49,495
16	17,00,000	19,60,000	5,52,000	2,33,964	2,76,035
17	20,60,833	31,85,280	9,01,411	5,40,003	6,37,106
18	35,20,000	28,13,127	8,21,340	81,593	92,462
19	11,00,000	15,03,000	4,40,000	75,000	68,000
20	42,50,000	39,89,222	11,96,766	3,49,212	4,12,007
21	17,70,000	20,00,000	6,50,000	20,000	4,50,000
22	35,30,000	32,01,897	10,80,121	2,74,581	3,23,956
23	11,60,000	15,02,594	5,62,269	75,000	68,690
Avg =	17,66,244	26,12,660	5,98,785	1,90,123	3,27,916

Regression

Input

Input Y Range: $C$4:$C$26

Input X Range: $D$4:$G$26

☐ Labels ☐ Constant is Zero

☐ Confidence Level: 95 %

Output options

◉ Output Range: L1

○ New Worksheet Ply:

○ New Workbook

Residuals

☑ Residuals ☐ Residual Plots

☐ Standardized Residuals ☐ Line Fit Plots

? ✕

OK

Cancel

Help

EXHIBT 10.11 Multiple Variable Regressions

Source: Used with permission from Microsoft Corporation

131

SUMMARY OUTPUT

Regression Statistics	
Multiple R	0.949825
R Square	0.902168
Adjusted R Square	0.880428
Standard Error	363055.8
Observation	23

ANOVA

	df	SS	MS	F
Regression	4	2.1879E+13	5.47E+12	41.4973
Residual	18	2.3726E+12	1.32E+11	
Total	22	2.4252E+13		

	Coefficients	Standard Error	t Stat	P-value
Intercept	-738640	279458.304	-2.64311	0.016528
X Variable 1	0.102156	0.12022711	0.849692	0.406656
X Variable 2	3.93356	0.3840132	10.24329	6.16E-09
X Variable 3	-1.19358	0.57344791	-2.08141	0.051945
X Variable 4	0.334101	0.38170417	0.875288	0.392947

Independent Variable Coefficients

RESIDUAL OUTPUT

Observation	Predicted Y	Residuals
1	398034.2	51965.7867
2	1284500	-344500
3	1149029	-159028.75
4	502995.4	27187.5931

EXHIBIT 10.12   Continued-Multiple Variable Regressions

equipment variables. Note how all four columns of data are referenced in the "Input X Range" field. The data array is defined as $D$4:$G$26. Hence, we have selected columns D, E, F, and G starting at row 4 and continuing down to row 26.

It is important that all four columns for the X inputs are contiguous. There cannot be any blank columns separating the four columns of variables, nor can there be any blank cells in the array (i.e., no data).

If there are any blank cells or columns separating the data, the regression utility will return an error message. If you find a blank cell in the data, you may enter a zero in the cell to make the regression function properly. Just keep in mind that more than a couple of zeros in your columns of data will have a tendency to skew the final results.

The printout for the regression above and the location of the coefficients for the four variables in the regression equation are as follows:

In the exhibit the revenue coefficient is 0.10216, the cash flow (SDE) coefficient is 3.93356, the inventory coefficient is −1.19358, and the fixtures coefficient is 0.33410. Also note that the R^2 is 0.9021682 and the standard error is 363,056.

PRODUCTION VALUE OF EXCEL

By now you are aware that I am a firm believer that charts and diagrams are an integral part of one's appraisal report. They add a significant production value to an appraisal. Unfortunately, building charts and graphs for a report is time consuming. As such, they are often omitted. The regression utility is capable of creating dazzling graphs that can be updated instantly as new data is entered in the adjoining tables.

After we set up our columns of data for the transactions in our sample, we initiated the regression utility by accessing the regression utility widow (as shown in Exhibit 10.9). The "Regression" window had a check box for "Line Fit Plots." That option will create the graph shown below. Initially it is in a very rough form,

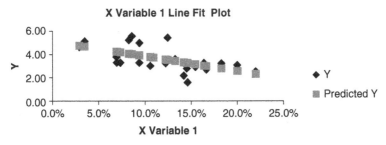

EXHIBIT 10.13 Regression Charts

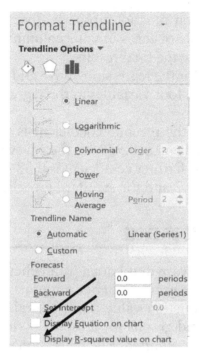

EXHIBIT 10.14   Trendline

but it can be reformatted similarly to all the graphs displayed throughout this book for a high-quality appearance. First, I recommend right-clicking on one of the brown square dots that are the predicted Ys and deleting them. Then, right-click on any of the blue dots and select the "add trendline" options window shown on Exhibit 10.14. Check off the "Display Equation on chart" box and the "Display R-squared value on chart." Close out the window, and the regression trendline, regression equation, and R^2 will now appear on your graph.

In Exhibit 10.13 you will note there are four text boxes, one on each side of the graph, that can be edited with more specific data. The boxes are labeled "X Variable 1," "Y," "X Variable 1 Line Fit Plots," and "Predicted Y." Click on each of the first three boxes and change the text to more relevant descriptions. For example, on one of my charts I changed the "X Variable" box to "SDE%"; the "Y" box to "Revenue Multipliers," and the "X Variable 1" box to "Regression Multipliers." The fourth text box, "Predicted Y," can be deleted to reduce the width of the graph. Finally, you can right-click on any of the borders of the graph and colorize them or make them bolder. Right-click anywhere in the center of the graph and you can add color or grid lines to the chart area.

Once you create this chart in a more desirable format, it can be reused as a template for future regressions. In the example below, the chart is permanently linked to the columns of data in H31:H54 and J31:J54 (or, wherever your columns of variable data were located). You can change the data in these columns for future regressions, and the linked chart will immediately be reformatted to reflect the new data.

The two data columns in Exhibit 10.15 become a permanent link to the graph that appears to the left of the two columns.

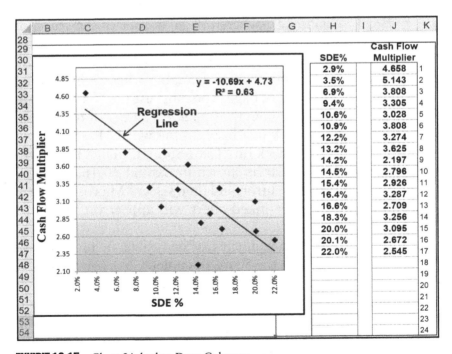

EXHIBIT 10.15 Chart Linked to Data Columns

Data for future samples can be entered into the two columns, and the graph will immediately be reconfigured to the new data and the linear equation and the R^2 will be recalculated. The graph portion of the exhibit can be moved anywhere independent of the two columns of data. The links between the graph and the data columns are permanently embedded into the graph.

The graph portion of the above exhibit can be copied/pasted into another worksheet, and more importantly, it can be pasted into a Word document, and the chart will still link back to the data in the original columns you created in the Excel file. This has a tremendous value for dressing up one's Word template with numerous graphs. The graphs will all link back to the Excel template where the data can be quickly changed for a new subject valuation. The Word graph will, then, automatically be updated with the new Excel information.

The following steps must be taken to paste an Excel graph into a Word document. Start by right-clicking anywhere on the border of the graph in Excel and select "Copy." Open the Word document where you wish to paste the chart. **Do not use the "Paste" option available when right-clicking on the Word page.** You must use the "Paste" drop-down menu in the upper left corner of the screen. Click on the little arrow just beneath the word "Paste." From the drop-down menu, click on "Paste Special." The "Paste Special" window will appear as shown in Exhibit 10.16. Click on the "Paste Link" radio button and then select "Microsoft Office Graphic Object." Your linked chart will appear on the Word document.

The document can be resized or moved anywhere on the Word document, but you must first do the following. Click anywhere on the chart and the icon shown on the left will appear on the upper right corner of the chart. Click on the icon and choose how you want the text to wrap around your chart just as you see it wrapping around the icon in this paragraph. The icon option has a dozen settings to fine-tune

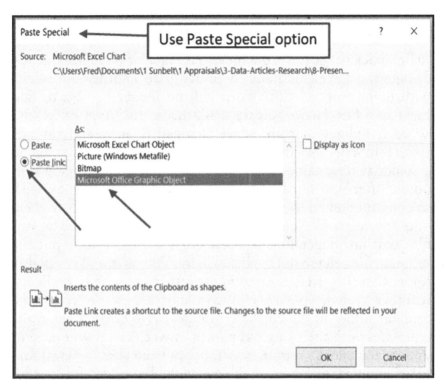

EXHIBIT 10.16   Paste Special Option

the positioning of your chart. If desired, right-click anywhere on the graph and select options for formatting, sizing, or positioning the graph.

The chart on the Word document is now permanently linked to the Excel document you created. Any changes on the Excel document will be changed automatically on the Word document. On occasion the Word document will fail to update. It can be manually updated by clicking on the document and hitting F9 on the keyboard. To be doubly safe that all the changes you made to the Excel template are updated in the Word document, go to "File" on the menu ribbon; then, take the path Options\Display\Printing Options and select "Update Linked objects before printing." This option will assure that all linked charts on your Word document are updated before you print out the report.

A word of caution regarding linking Excel and Word. The Word document embeds the complete path name for the graph to link back to the Excel document. As such, if you subsequently change the Excel file name or move it to another folder, the path name embedded in Word will no longer be able to find the Excel file. Hence, create a file name for your Excel and Word templates that are never changed or moved (Example: ExcelTemplate.xlsx and WordTemplate.docx) and keep them in a folder with a name like "Template." For housekeeping purposes, after you finish a report for one client you may wish to copy the linked Word and Excel documents and paste them into another folder named for your client's company. The two files will no longer link to each other in that folder, but the original files that you copied will remain in the "Template" folder that they were created in for future use with new clients. In other words, you must always start a new project in the original folder in which the templates were created using the templates with their original names. If weeks later you need to update the client's report, you must put the client's Word and Excel template files back in the original "Template" folder and, if necessary, change the file names back to their original template names. Make whatever changes you need to make to the linked templates, print out the updated report, and then copy the updated files back into the client's folder.

Yes, it is cumbersome. But the linking of templates is so powerful that the inconveniences of file name changes is worth it. I link P&Ls between the Excel and Word files. If the client hands me an updated P&L a week after I finished the report, it is a simple task to update the spreadsheet, and the Word document is updated automatically. I usually have up to 1,000 linked objects in my templates that enable the Word document to be completely rewritten when financials or other information are updated weeks or months later.

There is a utility that will enable you to re-assign the Word template links to a renamed Excel file. In true Excel fashion, it is slow and cumbersome. After you move the two templates to a new folder with the client's name, you can re-assign the Word links to the Excel files in that folder.

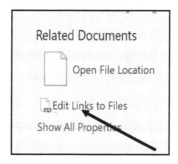

EXHIBIT 10.17 Edit Links

First, click on "File" on the left side of the main menu ribbon. The "INFO" menu window will pop up. In the lower right-hand corner of the screen click on the "Edit Links to Files" option.

The window lists all the linked charts in your Word document and the path name to the Excel file to which it is presently linked. Click on a file path name that you wish to reassign such

Links				? ✕
Source file	Item	Type	Update	
C:\...\Formal-Inc...	Data!R15C10	Excel.SheetMacroEnable...	Man	**Update Now**
C:\...\Formal-Inc...	Data!R4C1	Excel.SheetMacroEnable...	Auto	
C:\...\Formal-Inc...	Data!R9C5	Excel.SheetMacroEnable...	Auto	**Open Source**
C:\...\Formal-Inc...	Data!R7C5	Excel.SheetMacroEnable...	Auto	
C:\...\Formal-Inc...	Data!R16C9	Excel.SheetMacroEnable...	Auto	
C:\...\Formal-Inc...	Data!R15C10	Excel.SheetMacroEnable...	Auto	**Change Source...**
C:\...\Formal-Inc...	Data!R15C11	Excel.SheetMacroEnable...	Auto	
C:\...\Formal-Inc...	Data!R14C10	Excel.SheetMacroEnable...	Auto	**Break Link**
C:\...\Formal-Inc...	Data!R4C5	Excel.SheetMacroEnable...	Auto	

Source information for selected link

Source file: C:\...\a-Market Approach\Formal-Inc-Mkt-Sgl Per Equity-Pedrick Produce-V69.xlsm

Item in file: Data!R15C10

Link type: Microsoft Excel Macro-Enabled Worksheet

Update method for selected link

○ Automatic update

● Manual update

☐ Locked

Options for selected link

☑ Save picture in document

☑ Preserve formatting after update

[OK] [Cancel]

EXHIBIT 10.18 Change Source

as the one highlighted in blue (gray in this exhibit). Next, click "Change Source." The standard File Explorer window will pop up as shown in the exhibit below. Search for the new Excel file you wish to link to the Word document. Once you find that Excel file in your client's folder, click on that file name and the chart in Word will now be linked to that Excel File.

You will have to do the same steps for each linked chart that you have in your Word template. As I mentioned earlier, it is just easier to move the Excel and Word templates to the desired new folder. If you have to update the two templates, merely put them back in the original folder where they were created and change their file names to the original names.

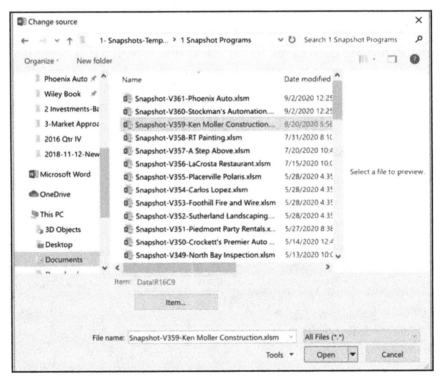

EXHIBIT 10.18   Selecting Source to Change

CHAPTER 11

Excel Valuation Template

This chapter will include screenshots of the eight Excel worksheets that comprise the regression template that is included with the purchase price of this book. Literally everything you learned about the regression methodology presented here will be implemented by the click of a button in the blink of an eye.

WORKSHEET #1: DATA ENTRY

The first worksheet in the template is the "Data Entry" worksheet. At the minimum you will need to fill in columns a, b, and c in Exhibit 11.1 with the transactional data for selling price, revenue, and SDE cash flow. If your subject carries inventory as a major source of revenue, I highly recommend filling out column d with inventory data. As was discussed in Chapter 9, if the subject generates a significant portion of its revenue from the sale of inventory (retail, wholesale, or manufacturers are most common), it is critically important to select only those comparables that reported that inventory was sold. Do not use comparables that indicate that no inventory was transferred in the sale.

ABC Machine Shop

	Selling Price (a)	Gross Revenues (b)	Cash Flow (SDE) (c)	Inventory (d)	Fixtures (e)	SDE% c + b	Revenue Multiplier a ÷ b	Cash Flow Multiplier a ÷ c	Enterprise Multiplier (a-d) ÷ b	Sort By SDE%
1	4,50,000	29,71,358	2,33,651	1,00,000	1,00,000	7.9%	0.15	1.93	0.12	Hide Inventory Columns
2	9,40,000	37,05,000	4,04,000	40,000	3,09,000	10.9%	0.25	2.33	0.24	
3	9,90,000	35,00,000	4,27,841	1,87,510	2,12,489	12.2%	0.28	2.31	0.23	
4	5,30,183	18,01,092	2,54,321	50,000	3,50,000	14.1%	0.29	2.08	0.27	Hide Fixtures Column
5	7,66,959	22,33,258	3,31,424	3,61,630	4,26,657	14.8%	0.34	2.31	0.18	
6	13,95,000	29,30,376	4,96,820	40,947	48,310	17.0%	0.48	2.81	0.46	
7	22,08,692	36,20,708	6,67,675	2,69,471	3,17,928	18.4%	0.61	3.31	0.54	Show All Columns
8	15,10,022	23,86,283	4,58,137	1,10,022	6,00,000	19.2%	0.63	3.30	0.59	
9	13,00,000	19,00,000	3,85,000	1,83,501	2,16,498	20.3%	0.68	3.38	0.59	
10	15,66,925	28,01,382	6,68,522	5,12,393	6,04,531	23.9%	0.56	2.34	0.38	
11	9,25,000	15,28,734	3,72,403	38,490	45,412	24.4%	0.61	2.48	0.58	
12	35,00,000	34,04,875	8,81,344	1,23,000	9,69,482	25.9%	1.03	3.97	0.99	
13	17,00,000	25,33,000	6,93,000	1,26,000	50,000	27.4%	0.67	2.45	0.62	
14	11,50,000	17,20,000	4,80,000	30,000	3,14,000	27.9%	0.67	2.40	0.65	CLEAR OLD DATA
15	26,00,000	29,00,000	8,14,000	5,50,504	6,49,495	28.1%	0.90	3.19	0.71	
16	17,00,000	19,60,000	5,52,000	2,33,964	2,76,035	28.2%	0.87	3.08	0.75	
17	20,60,833	31,85,280	9,01,411	5,40,003	6,37,106	28.3%	0.65	2.29	0.48	
18	35,20,000	28,13,127	8,21,340	81,593	92,462	29.2%	1.25	4.29	1.22	
19	11,00,000	15,03,000	4,40,000	75,000	68,000	29.3%	0.73	2.50	0.68	
20	42,50,000	39,89,222	11,96,766	3,49,212	4,12,007	30.0%	1.07	3.55	0.98	
21	17,70,000	20,00,000	6,50,000	20,000	4,50,000	32.5%	0.89	2.72	0.88	
22	35,30,000	32,01,897	10,80,121	2,74,581	3,23,956	33.7%	1.10	3.27	1.02	
23	11,60,000	15,02,594	5,62,269	75,000	68,690	37.4%	0.77	2.06	0.72	
	17,66,244	26,12,660	5,98,785	1,90,123	3,27,916	SDE % Range	Revenue Mult Range	Cash Flow Mult Range	Cash Flow Mult Range	
				Lower Quartile		17.7%	0.52	2.32	0.42	
				Median		25.9%	0.67	2.50	0.59	
				Upper Quartile		28.8%	0.88	3.29	0.74	

Company Information

Report Date:	March 8, 2020
Prepared For:	John Smith
Company Name:	ABC Machine Shop
Address:	123 Any Street
City, State:	Anytown, CA

Financial Data

Valuation As Of:	December 31, 2019
Revenue:	$22,92,000
Cash Flow (SDE):	$5,50,000
Current Inventory:	$1,30,000
Current Fixtures:	

EXHIBIT 11.1   Excel Template—Data Entry Worksheet

If you wish to include the multiple variable regression analysis in the final reconciliation of values, then fill in column e with the fixtures and equipment data. If you do not wish to include inventory or fixtures in the table, click the "Hide Inventory Columns" or "Hide Fixtures Column." You can unhide them later if you change your mind.

Lastly, at the bottom of the worksheet you must fill in the subject company's contact information and the financial information. The financial data for revenue and cash flow can be any year or an average of any number of years that you consider appropriate to value the subject.

WORKSHEETS #2–4: REVENUE, SDE, AND ENTERPRISE MULTIPLIERS

Exhibit 11.4 to Exhibit 11.6 are the next three worksheets in the template. The first worksheet shows the revenue multiplier regression; the second, the cash flow multiplier regression; and the third, the enterprise multiplier regression. The top graph on each worksheet shows the first-level regression of the multipliers. The bottom chart shows the second regression with the outliers removed. All you need to do here *on each worksheet* is click on the "Click to Reformat Charts" button. Within less than a second, the two charts on each worksheet are reformatted showing the regressions for the multipliers from the data that you entered on the "Data Entry" worksheet. All the outliers are automatically identified and highlighted in yellow (shaded gray in the exhibit). The bottom chart is also produced immediately showing the second regression with the outliers removed. There is nothing you

Click to Reformat Charts

EXHIBIT 11.2   Excel Template-Revenue Multiplier Regression

Polynomial Regression	
Trendline	**Enterprise Multiplier**
Linear	Enterprise Linear
Curved	Enterprise Curved

EXHIBIT 11.3   Curved Option

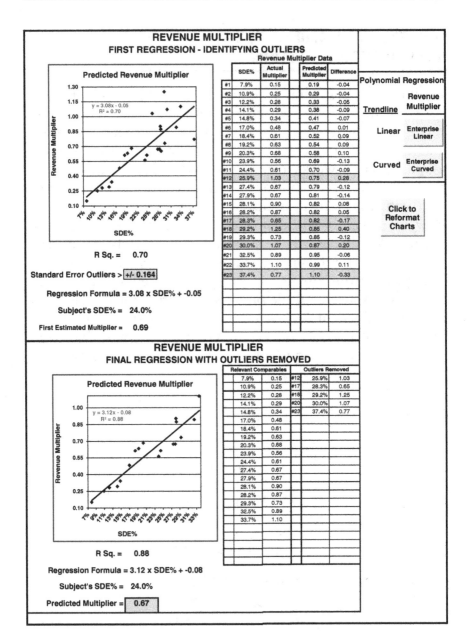

REVENUE MULTIPLIER
FIRST REGRESSION - IDENTIFYING OUTLIERS

Revenue Multiplier Data

	SDE%	Actual Multiplier	Predicted Multiplier	Difference
#1	7.9%	0.15	0.19	-0.04
#2	10.9%	0.25	0.29	-0.04
#3	12.2%	0.26	0.33	-0.05
#4	14.1%	0.29	0.38	-0.09
#5	14.8%	0.34	0.41	-0.07
#6	17.0%	0.48	0.47	0.01
#7	18.4%	0.61	0.52	0.09
#8	19.2%	0.63	0.54	0.09
#9	20.3%	0.68	0.58	0.10
#10	23.9%	0.56	0.69	-0.13
#11	24.4%	0.61	0.70	-0.09
#12	25.9%	1.03	0.75	0.28
#13	27.4%	0.67	0.79	-0.12
#14	27.9%	0.67	0.81	-0.14
#15	28.1%	0.90	0.82	0.08
#16	28.2%	0.87	0.82	0.05
#17	28.3%	0.65	0.82	-0.17
#18	29.2%	1.25	0.85	0.40
#19	29.3%	0.73	0.85	-0.12
#20	30.0%	1.07	0.87	0.20
#21	32.5%	0.89	0.95	-0.06
#22	33.7%	1.10	0.99	0.11
#23	37.4%	0.77	1.10	-0.33

Predicted Revenue Multiplier

$y = 3.08x - 0.05$
$R^2 = 0.70$

R Sq. = 0.70

Standard Error Outliers > +/- 0.164

Regression Formula = 3.08 x SDE% + -0.05

Subject's SDE% = 24.0%

First Estimated Multiplier = 0.69

Polynomial Regression

Revenue Multiplier

Trendline

Linear — Enterprise Linear

Curved — Enterprise Curved

Click to Reformat Charts

REVENUE MULTIPLIER
FINAL REGRESSION WITH OUTLIERS REMOVED

Relevant Comparables		Outliers Removed		
7.9%	0.15	#12	25.9%	1.03
10.9%	0.25	#17	28.3%	0.65
12.2%	0.26	#18	29.2%	1.25
14.1%	0.29	#20	30.0%	1.07
14.8%	0.34	#23	37.4%	0.77
17.0%	0.48			
18.4%	0.61			
19.2%	0.63			
20.3%	0.68			
23.9%	0.56			
24.4%	0.61			
27.4%	0.67			
27.9%	0.67			
28.1%	0.90			
28.2%	0.87			
29.3%	0.73			
32.5%	0.89			
33.7%	1.10			

Predicted Revenue Multiplier

$y = 3.12x - 0.08$
$R^2 = 0.88$

R Sq. = 0.88

Regression Formula = 3.12 x SDE% + -0.08

Subject's SDE% = 24.0%

Predicted Multiplier = 0.67

EXHIBIT 11.4 Excel Template–Revenue Multiplier Regression

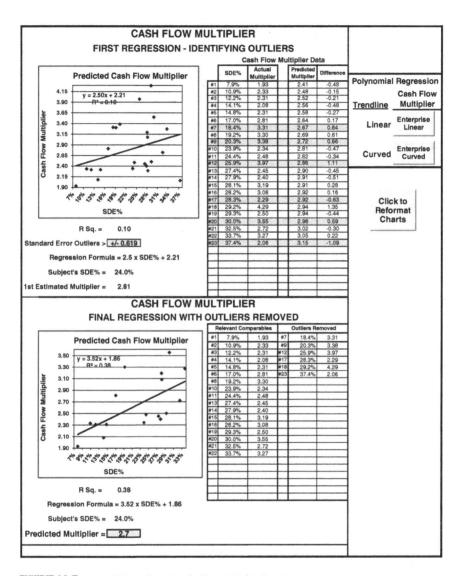

EXHIBIT 11.5 Excel Template-Cash Flow Multiplier Regression

need to do here. All the regression work on both charts in Exhibit 11.5 is accomplished with the click of that one button.

You will also notice in the upper right-hand corner of each worksheet two additional buttons. By clicking on the "Revenue Curved" button or the "Revenue Linear" button, you will be able to change the linear regressions into polynomial curved

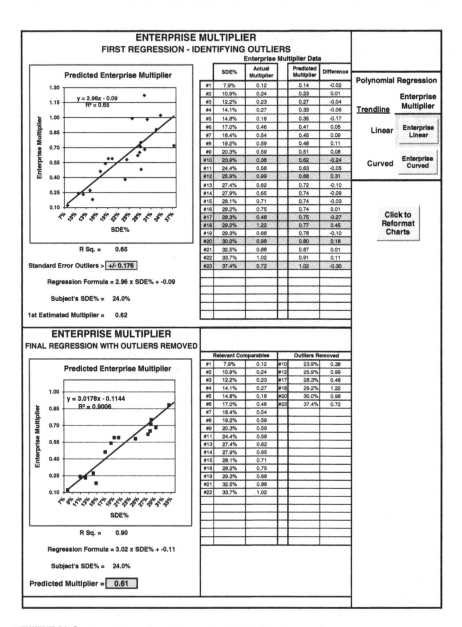

EXHIBIT 11.6   Excel Template–Enterprise Multiplier Regression

regressions. The two charts will instantly be reformatted with the curved regressions with the polynomial formulas and the corresponding R^2 displayed on each chart. If the results of the curved regressions do not appear to be reasonable to you or the R^2 hasn't improved, then click on the "Revenue Linear," "Cash Flow Linear," or "Enterprise Linear" buttons on the respective worksheets to return the two charts to linear formats. You may click on any combination of buttons as many times as you want. Nice!

WORKSHEET #5: TWO-LEVEL MULTIPLE REGRESSION

The next worksheet of the template, Exhibit 11.8, shows the two-level multiple variable regression analysis. If you did not enter any fixtures and inventory data for the samples' transactions on the first worksheet, then skip this worksheet. If you did enter that data, all you need to do on this worksheet is click on the "Run Multi-Variable Regression" button at the top of the worksheet. The button will run the first regression shown on the left side of the worksheet to identify all the outliers. The outliers will automatically be highlighted in yellow (shaded gray in the Exhibit). The results of the second regression with the outliers removed will appear within a few seconds on the right side of the worksheet. The outliers will be sorted to the table below the second regression.

Run Multi-Variable Regression

EXHIBIT 11.7 Excel Template-Final Reconciliation Worksheet-Two Methods

The data in the lower left corner of the worksheet will list the R^2 and the standard error of the first regression and the R^2 and standard error of the second regression. Finally, the regression formula calculated by the second regression will appear at the bottom of the worksheet in the following format:

Selling Price $= 0.029 \times \text{Rev} + 4.019 \times \text{SDE} + -0.903 \times \text{Inv}$

$+ 0.534 \times \text{Fix} + -684,195$

The above formula will be carried to the final reconciliation worksheet. The subject's financials that were entered on the "Data Entry" worksheet will be inserted into the formula automatically.

2-Level Multiple Variable Regression

First Multi-Variable Regression to IDENTIFY OUTLIERS

	Predicted Selling Price	Selling Price	Revenue	Cash Flow	Inventory	Fixtures	Outliers
1	3,98,034	4,50,000	29,71,358	2,33,651	1,00,000	1,00,000	
2	12,84,500	9,40,000	37,05,000	4,04,000	40,000	3,09,000	
3	11,49,029	9,90,000	35,00,000	4,27,841	1,87,510	2,12,489	
4	5,02,995	5,30,183	18,01,092	2,54,321	50,000	3,50,000	
5	5,04,089	7,66,959	22,33,258	3,31,424	3,61,630	4,26,657	
6	14,82,253	13,95,000	29,30,376	4,96,820	40,947	48,310	
7	20,42,162	22,08,692	36,20,708	6,67,675	2,69,471	3,17,928	
8	13,76,383	15,10,022	23,86,283	4,58,137	1,10,022	6,00,000	
9	8,23,186	13,00,000	19,00,000	3,85,000	1,83,501	2,16,498	1
10	17,67,602	15,66,925	28,01,382	6,68,522	5,12,393	6,04,531	
11	8,51,630	9,25,000	15,28,734	3,72,403	38,490	45,412	
12	32,53,102	35,00,000	34,04,875	8,81,344	1,23,000	9,69,482	
13	21,12,392	17,00,000	25,33,000	6,93,000	1,26,000	50,000	2
14	13,94,277	11,50,000	17,20,000	4,80,000	30,000	3,14,000	
15	23,19,457	26,00,000	19,60,000	8,14,000	5,50,504	6,49,495	
16	14,45,880	17,00,000	19,60,000	5,52,000	2,33,964	2,76,035	
17	27,00,831	20,60,833	31,85,280	9,01,411	5,40,003	6,37,106	3
	27,13,031	35,20,000	28,13,127	8,21,340	81,593	92,462	4
15	10,78,867	11,00,000	15,03,000	4,40,000	75,000	68,000	
16	40,97,273	42,50,000	39,89,222	11,96,766	3,49,212	4,12,007	
	21,48,959	17,70,000	20,00,000	6,50,000	20,000	4,50,000	5
17	36,17,673	35,30,000	32,01,897	10,80,121	2,74,581	3,23,956	
	15,60,008	11,60,000	15,02,594	5,62,269	75,000	68,690	6

Second Multi-Variable Regression with OUTLIERS REMOVED

Run Multi-Variable Regression

	Predicted Selling Price	Selling Price	Revenue	Cash Flow	Inventory	Fixtures	Residual Difference
1	3,03,305	4,50,000	29,71,358	2,33,651	1,00,000	1,00,000	-1,46,695
2	11,74,804	9,40,000	37,05,000	4,04,000	40,000	3,09,000	2,34,804
3	10,79,993	9,90,000	35,00,000	4,27,841	1,87,510	2,12,489	89,993
4	5,31,451	5,30,183	18,01,092	2,54,321	50,000	3,50,000	1,268
5	6,13,331	7,66,959	22,33,258	3,31,424	3,61,630	4,26,657	-1,53,628
6	13,85,457	13,95,000	29,30,376	4,96,820	40,947	48,310	-9,543
7	20,29,640	22,08,692	36,20,708	6,67,675	2,69,471	3,17,928	-1,79,052
8	14,46,726	15,10,022	23,86,283	4,58,137	1,10,022	6,00,000	-63,296
9	19,43,297	15,66,925	28,01,382	6,68,522	5,12,393	6,04,531	3,76,372
10	8,45,852	9,25,000	15,28,734	3,72,403	38,490	45,412	-79,148
11	33,62,447	35,00,000	34,04,875	8,81,344	1,23,000	9,69,482	-1,37,553
12	14,34,909	11,50,000	17,20,000	4,80,000	30,000	3,14,000	2,84,909
13	25,20,392	26,00,000	19,60,000	8,14,000	5,50,504	6,49,495	-79,608
14	15,26,731	17,00,000	19,60,000	5,52,000	2,33,964	2,76,035	-1,73,269
15	10,95,877	11,00,000	15,03,000	4,40,000	75,000	68,000	-4,123
16	41,44,811	42,50,000	39,89,222	11,96,766	3,49,212	4,12,007	-1,05,189
17	36,73,759	35,30,000	32,01,897	10,80,121	2,74,581	3,23,956	1,43,759

OUTLIERS

	Predicted Selling Price	Selling Price	Revenue	Cash Flow	Inventory	Fixtures	Residual Difference
1	8,23,186	13,00,000	19,00,000	3,85,000	1,83,501	2,16,498	-4,76,814
2	21,12,392	17,00,000	25,33,000	6,93,000	1,26,000	50,000	4,12,392
3	27,00,831	20,60,833	31,85,280	9,01,411	5,40,003	6,37,106	6,39,998
4	27,13,031	35,20,000	28,13,127	8,21,340	81,593	92,462	-8,06,969
5	21,48,959	17,70,000	20,00,000	6,50,000	20,000	4,50,000	3,78,959
6	15,60,008	11,60,000	15,02,594	5,62,269	75,000	68,690	4,00,008

First Regression R Squared: 0.902
Standard Error: +/- 363,056

Second Regression R Squared: 0.977 (Outliers removed)
Standard Error: +/- 195,924

Regression Formula with Outliers Removed:
Selling Price =
0.029 x Rev + 4.019 x SDE + -0.903 x Inv + 0.534 x Fix + -684,196

EXHIBIT 11.8 Excel Template – 2-Level Multiple Variable Regression

148

WORKSHEET #6: 36-LEVEL MULTIPLE REGRESSION

The next worksheet, Exhibit 11.10, is the 36-level regression analysis. Because of the size of the printout, the exhibit is shown on two pages. If you did not read the advanced regression methodology in Chapter 9 or you are not prepared to discuss t Stats and P-values if challenged, then skip this worksheet and stick with the 2-level multiple variable worksheet. However, if you only use the 2-level method, it is worth looking at the 36-level worksheet just as a "sanity check." Sometimes the 36-level analysis reveals some problems that we will discuss that the 2-level method didn't take into account. In this case, you may opt to abandon multiple variable regression altogether.

Run Regression Series

EXHIBIT 11.9 Excel Template-Final Reconciliation Worksheet—Four Methods

As in the prior regression worksheets, all you need to do here is click on the "Run Regression Series" button to run the regression. The 36 regressions will take about 30 seconds to run, and sometimes nothing will happen on your screen while Excel is running the utility. So be patient.

As we discussed in Chapter 9, the standard error is used to determine the break point by which transactions are identified as outliers. Beginning at the top of Exhibit 11.10, the four levels of regressions are initially run using a standard error of 1.0 (in other words 1.0 times the standard error). The printout ignores the first-level regression in each grouping since the entire sample is run with no outliers removed. The data for levels 2 to 4 identifies the number of outliers that were removed at each level. This is an important consideration because, ideally, we want our final sample to include as many of the relevant transactions as possible to give us the best indication of where the market is.

You will note the "Std Err Mult" column on the left side of the table with groupings from 1.0 to 1.9. The first

36-Level Multiple Variable Regression

Run Regression Series

Subject's Financials

Annual Revenues =	$22,62,262
Cash Flow (SDE) =	$5,08,000
Current Inventory =	$3,55,607
Current Fixtures =	$43,853

Regression Formula (Override)

Price =

Sales x 0.12 + SDE x 2.91 + Inv x 0.19 + FF&E x 0.69 + - 3,02,098 =

Override Value = **$15,45,273**

Override R Sq. = 0.85

To Override Enter X	Std Err Mult	Reg Level	a Total Sample	b Selected Observations	c Outliers	d	e R²	f R2R Rating	g Overall Rating P-Val + R2R	h Total P-Val	i P-Val Sales	j P-Val CF	k P-Val Inv	l P-Val FF&E	m P-Val Interc
	1.0	2	25	18	7		0.91	0.66 = $15,22,741	1.798	1.178	0.032	0.400	0.599	0.001	0.146
		3	25	14	11				Excessive Outliers						
		4	25	11	14				Excessive Outliers						
X	1.1	2	25	20	5	Sales x 0.12 + SDE x 2.91 + Inv x 0.19 + FF&E x 0.69 + (3,02,098) = $15,45,273	0.85	0.68 = $15,45,273	1.169	0.796	0.044	0.400	0.229	0.023	0.101
		3	25	17	8		0.94	0.64 = $13,99,594	1.787	1.147	0.003	0.000	0.778	0.000	0.366
		4	25	14	11				Excessive Outliers						
	1.2	2	25	20	5		0.85	0.68 = $15,45,273	1.462	0.996	0.044	0.600	0.229	0.023	0.101
		3		15	10			= $13,99,594	Duplicate Regression						
		4	25						Excessive Outliers						
	1.3	2	25	22	3		0.80	0.71 = $14,77,966	1.925	1.360	0.168	0.400	0.308	0.056	0.429
		3						= $13,99,594	Duplicate Regression						
		4	25				0.74	0.71 = $14,15,199	Duplicate Regression						
	1.4	2	25	24	1		0.74	0.74 = $14,40,681	1.560	1.111	0.251	0.000	0.156	0.123	0.581
		3	25	21	4	Sales x 0.11 + SDE x 3.16 + Inv x 0.25 + FF&E x 0.62 + (3,77,365) = $15,92,504	0.86	0.72 = $15,92,504	1.001	0.724	0.059	0.000	0.600	0.034	0.031
		4	25	19	6		0.91	0.69 = $15,93,326	1.600	1.102	0.066	0.400	0.600	0.003	0.033

EXHIBIT 11.10 Excel Template—36 Level Multiple Variable Regression

EXHIBIT 11.10 (Continued)

1.5	2											Duplicate Regression	= $15,70,853
	3											Duplicate Regression	= $15,00,568
	4											Duplicate Regression	= $14,63,154
1.6	2	0.74	25	24	1	1.556	1.108	0.251	0.000	0.156	0.120	0.581	= $14,40,681
	3											Duplicate Regression	= $14,40,681
	4	0.74										Duplicate Regression / 0.71	= $14,40,681
1.7	2	0.74	25	24	1	1.903	1.355	0.251	0.000	0.400	0.123	0.581	= $14,40,681
	3											Duplicate Regression	= $14,40,681
	4	0.74										Duplicate Regression / 0.71	= $14,40,681
1.8	2	0.74	25	24	1	2.113	1.505	0.251	0.000	0.550	0.123	0.581	= $14,40,681
	3											Duplicate Regression	= $1,89,677
	4											Duplicate Regression	= $1,89,677

151

four regressions are run in the 1.0 group using 1.0 times the standard error as the break point to identify outliers. Eight more groups are run with the standard error increased by 0.1 in each successive group. The last grouping, "1.9," used 1.9 × the standard error as the break point to identify the outliers. The reason for increasing the standard error break point is that we will be removing smaller slices of outliers at each level. The result may leave some of the transactions in the calculation that are close enough to the regression line to be considered relevant. Again, we would like to include as many relevant transactions in our sample as possible to give us the best indication of where the market is.

Column g in the center of the exhibits, entitled "Overall Rating," shows the rating that each regression earned. The regression with the lowest rating, highlighted in yellow (gray in the exhibit), is considered the best choice. Some of the regressions removed too many outliers to be considered relevant. Any regression with more than 33% of the transactions removed is considered unusable and is labeled "Excessive Outliers" in the "Overall Rating" column (column g).

On the far-right side of the exhibit, the data for the best regression is plugged into the subject's financial information. The formula for the best rating and the calculated value are displayed.

After reviewing the 36 different regressions, one may notice that the P-value for one of the coefficients was greater than 0.50. The P-values for these transactions are highlighted in light red (gray in the exhibit) to indicate they may not be good choices for the regression. Hence, for example, if your subject has a high level of fixtures and equipment and you observe that the P-value for fixtures is excessive, you may consider choosing the next best overall rating that has a P-value for fixtures that is less than 0.50.

In Exhibit 11.9 the regression in level #3–1.4 generated the lowest (best) overall rating (column g). Hence, the regression is highlighted in yellow (gray in the exhibit). However, we notice that the P-value for inventory (column k) is greater than 0.50, indicating that the calculation for inventory may not be accurate. Since our subject is heavily invested in inventory, we should consider looking for the regression with the next best overall rating that has an inventory P-value less than 0.50. In this instance, the regression with the second best overall rating was Level #2–1.1. Its overall rating was 1.169, which was just slightly higher (worse) than the best overall rating of 1.001. However, the P-value for inventory in the second-best regression was only 0.229, considerably lower (better) than the 0.60 P-value in the regression with the best overall rating.

Had we elected to use the two-level regression from the "MultiVariable" worksheet (worksheet #5), the resulting value would have been $1,522,741. However, the 36-level regression found that regression in level #2–1.0 had a high P-value of 0.599. Hence, the regression in level #2–1.1 produced a more credible value of $1,545,273.

To choose a regression that is different than the one selected by the regression utility, merely place an "x" in the far left-hand column next to the regression that you prefer. All the calculations and data on the right side of the worksheet will be recalculated with your chosen regression, and this data will be carried to the final reconciliation worksheet.

The 36-level regression printout has a large amount of data that one must comb through, which may make parsing the results slow and clumsy. Hence, to simplify the printout, some of the regression data is blanked out and the best ratings are color-coded to make identifying them easier.

Any regression that had more than 33% of the outliers removed is considered irrelevant. These regressions will be labeled "Excess Outliers" in column g, and the data will be blanked out. It is also common that many of the regressions from different standard error levels will have the same outliers removed as other regressions. The data from these regressions will be labeled "Duplicate Regression" in column g, and the data will be blanked out.

To assist one in selecting the best choice of regressions to use, various color codes are used to draw one's attention. The regression utility will automatically choose the regression with the best (lowest) overall rating in column g. The entire line for that regression will be highlighted in yellow. If one decides to choose a different regression by placing an "x" in the far left-hand column, the entire line for that regression will become highlighted in gold.

Regressions with the best R^2 in column e are highlighted in blue; the second best is highlighted in red, and the third best is highlighted in silver. The same color coding is used to identify the regressions with the three best (lowest) overall ratings in column g, and the three best (lowest) total P-values in column h. The individual P-values for each regression that are greater than 0.50 will be highlighted in light red to indicate that they may not produce accurate results.

WORKSHEET #7: RECONCILIATION OF VALUES—TWO-REGRESSION OPTION

The last worksheet is the final reconciliation sheet. It brings forward all the values that were calculated by the regressions in the second through sixth worksheets and the company data from the first worksheet. After reviewing the results, you may decide to change the linear regressions to curved or add or remove the two multiple variable regressions as often as you like. You can also change all the company financial data as often as you like until your final results look reasonable to you.

Exhibit 11.11 below shows the first option for the reconciliation worksheet. The reconciliation of value is determined by

ABC Machine Shop

Company Information

Prepared For:	March 8, 2020
	John Smith
Company Name:	ABC Machine Shop
Address:	123 Any Street
City, State:	Anytown, CA

Financial Data

Date of Valuation / Financial Statement Date: December 31, 2019

Annual Revenues =	$22,92,000	
Cash Flow (SDE) =	$5,50,000	SDE%
Current Inventory =	$1,30,000	24.0%
Current Fixtures =	$9,00,000	

Statistical Analysis of Sold Comparables

ABC Machine Shop's SDE % is 24%
The Subject is in the Middle Range of SDE%.

	Revenue Multiplier Range	Cash Flow Multiplier Range	Enterprise Multiplier Range
The Lowest 25% of Companies have SDE% of Less Than 15.4%	0.40	2.40	0.35
The Mid Range of Companies have SDE% of 22.1%	0.61	2.64	0.55
The Highest 25% of Companies have SDE% of More Than 28.1%	0.80	2.85	0.73

REVENUE MULTIPLIER VALUE

Regression Formula: SDE% x 3.12 + -0.081 = .67

R Sq. = 0.88

Multiplier		Revenue		Predicted Value		Weight
0.67	x	$22,92,000	=	$15,36,000	x	70.1%

Weighted Value $10,76,460

CASH FLOW MULTIPLIER VALUE

Regression Formula: SDE% x 3.522 + 1.86 = .2.7

R Sq. = 0.38

Multiplier		Cash Flow		Predicted Value		Weight
2.70	x	$5,50,000	=	$14,85,000	x	29.9%

Weighted Value $4,44,282

Probable Selling Price Including Inventory = $1,520,000

Click to
Show/Hide Enterprise Value

[Show/Hide Enterprise Value]

Click to
Show/Hide Multi-Variable regression

[Show/Hide]

Values Using Other Methodologies
(From Samples Worksheet Data)

Revenue Multipliers

Median
0.67
x 22,92,000
$15,35,640

Cash Flow Multipliers

Median
2.5
x 5,50,000
$13,75,000

Average of Above Multiplier Values $14,55,320

Spread between Above Multiplier Values $1,60,640

Spread between Regression Values $51,000

EXHIBIT 11.11 Excel Template-Final Reconciliation Worksheet-Two Methods

using just the revenue multiplier regression and the cash flow regression from the second and third worksheets. To the right of the reconciliation data is comparative data using medians and quartiles to determine the value of the business. This information is provided to show the user of the template how far off medians can be. (It will not appear on the printout of the worksheet.)

In the example illustrated in Exhibit 11.11, we see that the two regression values were only $51,000 apart, whereas the calculation of value using medians was $160,640 apart. The regression reconciliation produced a value of $1,520,000. The range of values using medians was $1,375,000 to $1,535,640 with an average median of $1,455,320. Given that the subject's SDE profit margin (SDE%) was 24% and the median of our sample was 22.1%, it is reasonable to conclude that the subject's value should fall somewhere above the median values, which it did.

WORKSHEET #7: RECONCILIATION OF VALUES—ENTERPRISE OPTION

The second option for the final reconciliation is shown on Exhibit 11.13. If the subject carries inventory that is a major source of its revenue, the enterprise multiplier should be included in the final reconciliation of value. However, you must have entered the inventory data for the transactions you listed on the "Data Entry" worksheet. By clicking on the "Show/Hide

| Show/Hide Enterprise Value |

Enterprise Value" button in the upper right-hand corner, you can determine if the enterprise value is worth including in the final reconciliation. You may click on the "Show/Hide" button as often

EXHIBIT 11.12   as you wish.

ABC Machine Shop

Company Information

Prepared For:	March 8, 2020
	John Smith
Company Name:	ABC Machine Shop
Address:	123 Any Street
City, State:	Anytown, CA

Financial Data

Date of Valuation / Financial Statement Date: December 31, 2019

		SDE%
Annual Revenues =	$22,92,000	24.0%
Cash Flow (SDE) =	$5,50,000	
Current Inventory =	$1,30,000	
Current Fixtures =	$8,00,000	

Statistical Analysis of Sold Comparables

ABC Machine Shop's SDE % is 24%
The Subject is in the Middle Range of SDE%.

		Revenue Multiplier Range	Cash Flow Multiplier Range	Enterprise Multiplier Range
The Lowest 25% of Companies have SDE% of	15.4%	0.40	2.40	0.35
The Mid Range of Companies han	22.1%	0.61	2.64	0.55
The Highest 25% of Companies have SDE% of	28.1%	0.80	2.85	0.73

REVENUE MULTIPLIER VALUE
Regression Formula: SDE% x 3.12 + -0.081 = .0.67   R Sq. .88

Multiplier		Revenue		Predicted Value		Weight		
0.67	x	$22,92,000	=	$15,35,640	x	40.8%	=	Weighted Value $6,26,803

CASH FLOW MULTIPLIER VALUE
Regression Formula: SDE% x 3.522 + 1.86 = .2.7   R Sq. = 0.38

Multiplier		Cash Flow		Predicted Value		Weight		
2.70	x	$5,50,000	=	$14,85,000	x	17.4%	=	Weighted Value $2,58,697

ENTERPRISE MULTIPLIER VALUE
Regression Formula: SDE% x 3.018 + -0.114 = .0.61   R Sq. = 0.9

Multiplier		Revenue		Inventory		Predicted Value		Weight		
0.61	x	$22,92,000	+	$1,30,000	=	$15,28,100	x	41.8%	=	Weighted Value $6,38,315

Probable Selling Price Including Inventory = $1,520,000

Click to
Show/Hide Enterprise Value
[Show/Hide Enterprise Value]

Click to
Show/Hide Multi-Variable regression
[Show/Hide Multi Regression]

Values Using Other Methodologies
(From Samples Worksheet Data)

Revenue Multipliers

	Median
	0.67
	x 22,92,000
	$15,35,640

Cash Flow Multipliers

	Median
	2.5
	x 5,50,000
	$13,75,000

Average of Above Multiplier Values $14,55,320
Spread between Above Multiplier Values $1,60,640
Spread between Regression Values $54,400

EXHIBIT 11.13 Excel Template–Final Reconciliation Worksheet–Three Methods

WORKSHEET #7: RECONCILIATION
OF VALUES—MULTIPLE VARIABLE OPTION

The final option one has for the reconciliation worksheet is to include the multiple variable regression data. This option requires that the transactional data entered in the "Data Entry" worksheet must include inventory and fixtures and equipment values. The best regression results will be achieved by selecting only those transactions that reported both asset values. Any missing data must be assumed to be a $0 value in order for the regression to work. Just be aware that a $0 value will have a tendency to skew one's results.

Show/Hide Multi Regression

By clicking on the "Show/Hide Multi Regression" button we can include the results for the multiple variable regression in the final reconciliation of value. After clicking on the "Show/Hide" button and selecting "show regressions," you will be given two options.

EXHIBIT 11.14

You may choose to show the data from the 2-level regression from the fifth worksheet or the data from the 36-level regression from the sixth worksheet.

In Exhibit 11.15 we find that adding the regression methodology to the final reconciliation increased the subject's value by $90,000. Was this a reasonable outcome? The subject carried $800,000 worth of fixtures and equipment, whereas the average transaction in our sample carried less than half that. The additional $400,000 in fixtures added $90,000 in value. A review of the transactional data in our sample showed five companies with $600,000 to $952,000 in fixtures that sold for an average revenue multiple of 0.75. The increased value that the multiple variable regression added to our subject increased its revenue multiple to 0.71. Hence, the $90,000 increase in value determined by the four methodologies was entirely reasonable.

Using just the revenue multiplier and the cash flow multiplier methods to determine the value of a company can

ABC Machine Shop		
Company Information		**Financial Data**

	March 8, 2020	**Date of Valuation /** **Financial Statement Date:**	December 31, 2019	
Prepared For:	John Smith	Annual Revenues =	$22,92,000	SDE%
Company Name:	ABC Machine Shop	Cash Flow (SDE) =	$5,50,000	24.0%
Address:	123 Any Street	Current Inventory =	$1,30,000	
City, State:	Anytown, CA	Current Fixtures =	$8,00,000	

Statistical Analysis of Sold Comparables

ABC Machine Shop's SDE % is 24% The Subject is in the Middle Range of SDE%.			Revenue Multiplier Range	Cash Flow Multiplier Range	Enterprise Multiplier Range
The Lowest 25% of Companies have SDE% of Less Than	15.4%	=	0.40	2.40	0.35
The Mid Range of Companies have SDE% of	22.1%	=	0.61	2.64	0.55
The Highest 25% of Companies have SDE% of More Than	28.1%	=	0.80	2.85	0.73

REVENUE MULTIPLIER VALUE

Regression Formula: SDE% x 3.12 + -0.081 = .0.67

R Sq. = 0.88

Multiplier		Revenue	Predicted Value	Weight		Weighted Value
0.67	x	$22,92,000	= $15,36,000 x	28.2%	=	$4,33,325

CASH FLOW MULTIPLIER VALUE

Regression Formula: SDE% x 3.522 + 1.86 = .2.7

R Sq. = 0.38

Multiplier		Cash Flow	Predicted Value	Weight		Weighted Value
2.70	x	$5,50,000	= $14,85,000 x	12.0%	=	$1,78,844

ENTERPRISE MULTIPLIER VALUE

Regression Formula: SDE% x 3.018 + -0.114 = .0.61

R Sq. = 0.9

Multiplier		Revenue		Inventory	Predicted Value	Weight		Weighted Value
0.61	x	$22,92,000	+	$1,30,000	= $15,28,100 x	28.9%	'=	$4,41,284

36-LEVEL MULTI-LEVEL REGRESSION VALUE

Price = Sales x 0.11 + SDE x 3.73 + Inv x -0.63 + FF&E x 0.64 + -861,593

R Sq. = 0.963

	Predicted Value	Weight		Weighted Value
=	$18,62,125	x	30.9%	$5,74,789

Probable Selling Price Including Inventory =	$1,630,000

EXHIBIT 11.15   Excel Template–Final Reconciliation Worksheet—Four Methods

occasionally miss the fact that it had a high level of assets compared to the transactions in the sample. Hence, the enterprise multiplier and the multiple variable regression become critical additions to the overall valuation process.

As we learned in Chapter 7, all the values calculated in the final reconciliation are weighted by their R^2 factors to arrive at the final conclusion of value. The inference is that those methods with a higher R^2 more accurately predicted the values of the transactions in the sample. Hence, they should be given a higher

EXHIBIT 11.16   Cover Sheet

weighting in the final reconciliation. In the example illustrated in Exhibit 11.10, the revenue multiplier value had an R^2 of 0.88, the cash flow multiplier an R^2 of 0.38, the enterprise multiplier an R^2 of 0.90, and the multiple variable regression an R^2 of 0.96. The total of all the R^2s is 3.12. Hence, the revenue multiplier was weighted 0.88/3.12, or 28.2%, the cash flow multiplier 0.38/3.12, or 12.0%, the enterprise multiplier 0.90/3.12, or 28.9%, and the multiple variable regression 0.98/3.12, or 30.9%.

WORKSHEET #8: COVER SHEET

The final page of the template is a little window dressing. All you need to do is paste your logo at the top, then copy a picture of the subject business from Google's man-on-the-street map, and you have a nice five- to seven-page valuation for your client.

CHAPTER 12

Conclusion

I am convinced that there are as many appraisal methodologies out there as there are appraisers and business brokers. Sadly, it would appear that many analysts start the assignment by asking the client, "How much do you want for it?" Then, the analyst becomes creative in producing a methodology that supports the desired conclusion of value. The Internet is rife with websites offering valuation tools that one can use to estimate the value of his or her business. These website tools range in cost from less than one hundred dollars to several thousand dollars.

All this has led the appraisal profession to treat the Market Approach as the red-headed stepchild in the appraisal industry. It seldom gets any attention, and values generated by all these methods are often discarded as irrelevant.

The Institute of Business Appraisers (IBA) began collecting market data for small business sales more that three decades ago, and Jack Sanders, the author of Bizcomps, began collecting sales data shortly thereafter. Initially, a minor amount of data was collected on each sale of a business, and there were few standards applied to the form of that data. Hence, the selling price of a business often included real estate, accounts receivable, cash, motor homes, assumed debt, and all sorts of non-business assets. The value of cash flow submitted by brokers ranged from gross profits, EBITDA, EBIT, owner's salary, SDE, or net profit after taxes with no distinction among any of them—they were all labeled "cash flow."

Hence, the quality of data was so poor that any attempt at developing a sophisticated quantitative methodology was doomed from the start. The use of the median was the only approach that made sense at the time. If one collected a sample of 25 transactions and sorted their revenue multipliers from the largest to the smallest, transaction #13 would be in the middle of the range of values; consequently, its value would be considered the median. There would be 12 transactions with higher multipliers than #13 and there would be 12 transactions with multipliers less than #13. The beauty of the median, therefore, is that it ignores all of the higher and lower transaction multipliers, no matter how good or bad they might be. A transaction's selling price may have included real estate, accounts receivable, or a vacation condo, but if its multiplier was not the median value of the sample, it was an outlier by definition. Hence, out of a sample of 25 transactions, the median technically eliminates 24 transactions as outliers.

Unfortunately, the median not only eliminates all the seriously flawed data, but it also eliminates all the truly relevant data. The revenue multipliers from two samples of similar companies might look something like this:

Sample	A	B
#1	0.23	0.58
#2	0.23	0.36
#3	0.23	0.35
#4	0.23	0.30
#5	0.23	0.21
#6	0.20	0.20
#7	0.19	0.08
#8	0.18	0.05
#9	0.17	0.04
#10	0.16	0.02
#11	0.15	0.01

The median multiplier of both samples is transaction #6—0.20, the midpoint of the range of values. The average of the two samples is also 0.20. Clearly, simple statistical tools can be very misleading. Sample B is loaded with what appears to be outliers. The range of multipliers in sample B is so great that one cannot suggest with any confidence that a multiplier of 0.20 is a reasonable conclusion, even though the sample's median and average are both 0.20. Regardless, a broker or appraiser would have no problem with selecting 0.20 as the choice of multipliers; it is, after all, the median value. However, sample A has so many transactions with a multiplier of 0.23, one might consider selecting 0.23 as the appropriate multiplier, and no one would challenge the choice. Occam's Razor, the principle that states, "The simplest solution is usually the right one," fails here.

Thirty years ago, Wall Street's quantitative analysis of a business was a quantum leap in sophistication over main street business analysis. Publicly traded companies produced volumes of financial data each quarter that were rigidly standardized. Public companies wanted their bottom line to look as good as possible to enhance the value of their stock. Main street companies were so small that most owners did their own books and very few of them understood accounting. As such, there was no standardization of the financial data produced by companies within the same industry. The owners also wanted to reduce the bottom line as much as possible to save income taxes. Wall Street companies had powerful mainframe computers that could crunch millions of bits of data in minutes. Main street business owners had a 10-key calculator.

My past career as an Ace Hardware dealer is a classic example. Back in the 1990s, Ace corporate wanted to develop a manual of best practices as recommendations for its dealers to help improve their bottom lines. However, Ace corporate had no idea what its 5,200 dealers were doing. There was no standardization of bookkeeping among the dealers. Some dealers buried warehouse labor, depreciation, or credit card charges in the cost of goods sold section. Others showed them as operating expenses. Hence, gross profit margins varied significantly from dealer to dealer even though they may have marked up their merchandise using the same percentage. Labor expense on the P&Ls also varied significantly because some dealers buried a portion of their labor expense in cost of goods sold, whereas other dealers showed all labor as an operating expense. Some dealers paid rent; others owned their property and paid no rent. The simple solution was to establish uniform bookkeeping standards for its 5,200 dealers so that Ace could better understand and assist its dealers. Ace corporate introduced the concept at its annual convention in 1995. Never in Ace's 70-year history had it been faced with such a complete and resounding mutiny of its dealers. No one was willing to change accounting methods no matter what the benefit might be.

Fast-forward 25 years—desktop computers now have more power than mainframes did in the 1990s. Main street is catching up to Wall Street. The Income Approach used by professional appraisers today to value a small business has become a highly complex financial analysis that is often up to 200 pages in length. Very few people outside the profession really understand the methodology. I have submitted hundreds of such valuations to clients, and no one has ever read past the bottom of the first page where the value of the business was listed.

The Market Approach is a different story. The methodology hasn't changed much in the last 25 years. For the most part, we still use the same weak statistical tools to analyze horribly flawed data. But the simplicity of the method was its selling point. It didn't really matter that much to most business brokers. A very rough estimate of value was all the broker needed to list a business for sale. If the value was a little high or too low, it was not important because it was the buyer who put an offer on the table. As such, there was little incentive to develop any precision in the Market Approach methodology.

However, in recent years professional appraisers have been increasingly using market data obtained from various transactional databases in their valuations. These valuations were being submitted to banks, courts of law, and to the Internal Revenue Service. Those end users demanded accuracy. Failure to meet that mandate might find the appraiser being sued for malpractice.

Fortunately, the appraisal profession has put considerable pressure on the various databases to gather transactional data more accurately. More importantly, the profession demanded that the data be consistent. In other words, the financial data for each transaction, such as SDE and the selling price, must be calculated in a uniform manner. Over the last three years, Dealstats and ValuSource have invested considerable sums of money and time to clean up their respective databases and create uniform standards for brokers and appraisal professionals to submit transactional data.

Now that we can obtain transactional data that is consistent and accurate, it is time that we also step up our game on the statistical tools that we use to analyze that data. Regression analysis should be at the top of the list of tools.

About the Website

Thanks for purchasing this book. You may access the following resources provided for your use by visiting www .affordablebusinessvaluations.com and navigating to the "Pricing Services" page.

- Regression Template for Use in Valuations
- Fixtures Depreciated Replacement Cost Template
- How to Install and Use Excel's Regression Utility

The templates require a password to open, which will give you a one-year complementary license. Please email me for that password. I am also available by email to answer your questions or to solve any problems that may arise.

Thanks,
C. Fred Hall, III MBA, CBA, CVA
fred@fredhall.biz

Index